P
MASTER
THE ESSE
AN

CW00828027

"Michelle Vidal's book contains much needed gems of knowledge with a deeper understanding of where we are in the world today. Through her beautifully rendered writing, Michelle Vidal offers clarity and directness so the reader can receive her wisdom. Mastering Metaphysic takes each reader on a journey from understanding our infinite truth and connection to the God Source through our vast knowing of healing and development of our natural gifts of spirit. This book shall be repeatedly read as it continuously offers the seeds and fruits that will help many comprehend how to implement her metaphysical lessons for greater unfoldment toward enlightenment."

Brother Francis E. Revels-Bey, Founder of Circle of Grace 1

www.circleofgrace1.us

"Mastering Metaphysics, the Essential Foundations and Principles by Michelle Vidal is a must read. Her no-nonsense, authentic, and heart-centered approach encourages the reader to question outdated assumptions, challenge previous learnings, and embrace new ways of thinking. She brings humor which makes this an engaging read that touches you on the soul level. I highly recommend this book."

Dr. Barbra Portzline, CEO, Organizational Rebel

www.OrganizationalRebel.com

Mastering Metaphysics:

The Essential Foundations and Principles

DM Vidal

Editing and editorial assistance by Rosemary Nevara and Mary Fulton
Cover Design by Donna Davis
Interior Design by Maryann Sperry

Library of Congress-in-Publication Data

Vidal, DM
Mastering Metaphysics: The Essential Foundations and Principles

Paperback ISBN: 979-8-9863652-1-3
Ebook ISBN: 979-8-9863652-2-0
Library of Congress Control Number: 2022918811

I dedicate this book to all spiritual seekers who are confused by information overload and to all others who are walking the path of love and light.

TABLE OF CONTENTS

INTRODUCTION

My journey into Metaphysics started at the age of 14. I had officially left any ideas of attending an organized religion and had picked up my first books in the arena of paranormal, witchcraft, and, of course, the philosophy of metaphysics. I was reading books by Lobsang Rampa, Gina Cerminara, Emmett Fox, and Aleister Crowley. Thank goodness my father didn't believe in censoring what I read as long as what was being read didn't bring on mass chaos.

As my search began, my world opened up, and with that, I had a greater understanding of who I was. I learned each of us has a level of truth. My truth will be different from yours. This doesn't mean we can't hold some of the same truths, but because each of us comes from many lives lived in many different worlds, our experiences in those lives determine our understanding of truth. This book is meant to be the foundation upon which you build your truth.

No longer afraid of my gifts, I started to own them and began my official training at the Universal Church of the Holy Spirit. This was a metaphysical church started by the Physical Trance Medium Edward Yonkers, who passed away in the mid-'80s. However, I didn't officially begin my training with the church until the early '90s.

Metaphysics is best defined as the science and study of All. Metaphysics looks at every piece of information gathered from science (physical), religion (emotion), and from philosophy (spirit), and brings the information together to formulate truth in accordance with each individual's level of understanding. As we humans progress intellectually finding more truths presented by facts, we can theorize bringing more light philosophically and balancing it against the studied religions. Truth never changes, but our understanding does. Light dawns brighter as we come into those truths, and we can understand truth more clearly. More aspects of truth are revealed as our states of consciousness rise.

Throughout this book, you will read terminology and concepts that you may or may not agree with. Understand that each of us has our own vision of truth, predicated on our own understanding. Words like Angel vs Spirit Guide are truly just semantics. Reserving judgment of the use of our terminology and thinking someone must say and think as we do will slow our spiritual progression.

My thirsting quest for knowledge took me down many roads. I offer the following:

Within each of us is a small voice that tells us, "There is something more. I am something more." We continue each day searching for answers to questions we didn't even know we had. Who we are is more than just the physical form of our bodies and the governing minds. Religion tells us we are "of the Father." We are taught the Father is God. The Who, What, Where, Why and the How of God is as individualized to each of us as is the decorations in our homes. Just like our tastes in decor, our ideas of God are stylized after our tastes and understandings of spiritual aesthetics.

How, then, do we find answers that resonate within us? Each time we come across someone who has found peace with their beliefs, their peace feeds the yearning to find that within and for ourselves. The question begs to be answered, "What does this person know and how did she/he find it so easy for themselves?" We ask, and hopefully, they will share their stories. Like a good book, we open the cover only to find the story is an old one told and retold through the generations as the only truth to life everlasting and peace on Earth. Yet, we no longer have an affinity for that story. It passed as we matured. When it speaks of damnation, if we are not in concurrence with the ultimate goal of raising our consciousness to reach truth in its purest form, it makes our skin crawl or, at the very least, it makes us sigh in frustration.

We step onward and hopefully, upward, searching and asking for the path to show itself. Again, we meet the person who seems to have all the answers. He/She speaks of the trials and tribulations found at the altar where they pray. The sacrifice of ideals under which we subjugate ourselves is done to gain spiritual knowledge and progression. Again, it doesn't resonate. We seek, only to find others who found an understanding of creation that works for them. Yet when they speak, they sound too far out to hold any level of truth in their words. It is as if the crystals hanging from their earlobes and around their necks are strangling their brains. Some of what they say sounds correct. You might liken it to "a bit of truth in an otherwise swirling hot pit of untruths." So we stop, study, and then crave more information. We reach for more truth, more light.

If this sounds like your journey, if any of what I say resonates within, then I welcome you. I offer my truth, to my highest and best ability, as I listen to your truth. I do this so that we may both progress to a higher, more fulfilled life. Thank you for showing up.

Namasté

UNIVERSAL AWARENESS

CHAPTER ONE

CREATION

The *Law of Conservation of Energy states, "Energy cannot be created or destroyed, only converted from one form into another; transferred from one object to another." Middle school and high school students are taught this as a fact in physical and physics science classes. When we understand this basic concept, we then understand there is perpetuity, eternity. When we take the physical form down to the molecular level, we understand we are nothing but matter. Everything consists of matter, and matter is made from atoms, which in turn are made up of protons, electrons, and neutrons which are in constant motion. Energy, simply put, is that which has the ability to do work. Your desk does not have the ability to do work; however, it holds potential energy. It has no movement to it, but your mind, body, and spirit can do work, therefore it is energy-matter.

*NOTE: There have been many changes in science since the time of these teachings. Quantum physics-subatomic particles, have all put a different definition on the nature of energy. To make this more scientifically correct, let's think of it as potential energy.

True Form of the God-Source

Children have asked, "What does God look like?" Christianity teaches we are made in his image, while still others give their God/ Goddesses human form crossed with an animal form. There is no definitive description. In Christianity, the supposition is God is a white, Caucasian male, who has two arms, two legs, a head, a mouth, a nose, walks upright, and sits on a throne. In the days this was taught, most people were uneducated. Visual eyesight, linear thinking, spiritual norms, and human ability or inability to comprehend gave us the concept that God is human in form, for the most part. Going one step further, because our physical father is male, the head of the household, our minds grasp the concept that God must have gender and be male. Artist renderings have continued this concept through the Judeo-Christian belief systems.

Our parents taught us what they were taught. We continue this traditional way of sharing knowledge when we teach our children about God. However, as we became more educated, and science brought forth discoveries of our world, a division was created between religion and science. Many people stand on their side of this division, refusing to open their minds to other possibilities. The Christian religion teaches the Bible is the only path to truth and salvation. Science says all matter was created during the Big Bang and life came about through evolution. We talk about the light of God, the light within, never once thinking this might be our true form as derived from the God-Source. Astrophysicist Neil deGrasse Tyson states in the first sentence of his book *Astrophysics for People in a Hurry,* "In the beginning, nearly fourteen billion years ago, all the space and all the matter and all the energy of the known universe was contained in a volume less than one-trillionth the size of the period that ends this sentence."

In the Beginning

As stated in the Introduction, these teachings are derived from the coursework given at the Universal Church of the Holy Spirit. Edwin Yonkers, a physical/trance medium, taught the information he gained through his many years of study and the high teachings of spirit through trance. Trance is a half-altered state reached through deep meditation.

In his teachings, Yonkers speaks of the Sea of Bliss. For clarity, I offer the Sea of Bliss is not heaven but the point of origin from which the universe was created and where the energy of the God-Source resides. The etheric is the dimension to which we return as we transition back to the other side when we leave our physical forms. The etheric is the place that many people define as heaven described in their religious teachings.

Within the Sea of Bliss resides the God-Source. The God-Source, Creator of The All, moved, and as it moved, it brought awareness of what it was to itself. The awareness of each individual particle of energy being a separate particle while at the same time making up the whole of the God-Source.

Taking it a step further, we see the energy changing, shifting as it draws near to other particles and away from still others. In one moment, we have the Big Bang, also known as the In-Breath of Brahma. As gaseous and liquid forms moved in this manner, they were created and solidified. This sent All That Is out into the Void, creating in the next moment the Universe of planets and galaxies. Because some particles vibrate at a different rate and awareness, we then have the creation of consciousness, each of which is different than the other such as in the different species of animals and plants.

The energy closest to the center of the God-Source vibrates higher in frequency, much like the ripples in a pond. The ripple circles start tight and spiral out quickly. In this manner, you can see how the universe unfurls or, mathematically, as a Fibonacci spiral. Understand this movement is very much like how our chakras flow. This imagery is evidenced by pictures of the galaxy. We see that as it moves outward from the center it becomes larger and moves more slowly.

The Elohim

The inside ripples or circles are where the hierarchy of angels resides. The Elohim stands as the first ripple and closest to the God-Source. They are the seven Orders of Angels in charge of our spinning wheels of energy called chakras. Each order has been assigned to a chakra center. Each chakra, also recognized as our spiritual centers, has a specific function. (We will talk more about our spiritual centers in another chapter.)

Lucifer was from the Order of Elohim. He was one of those in the first ripple, closest to the God-Source, the center of All That Is. It was Lucifer who brought to the other angels the thought we were just as good, just as powerful, just as all-knowing as the God-Source. We, as a part of the Seraphim Order, believed him and his thoughts. We rebelled and left the Sea of Bliss. Lucifer fell further than we did but did not lose his God Powers, powers we all held as a part of our beingness with the God-Source. Though his aura darkened, he never took on a physical body and therefore did not get caught up in the wheel of incarnation. Once he started to recognize and acknowledge truth, his aura started to lighten, and he is now back in the Sea of Bliss.

The Archangels

In the second ripple, or the next ring, are the archangels. There is not just one archangel such as Michael or Gabriel. The Archangels are in their own groups, and each archangel group has its own status and responsibilities.

The Michaels

The Michaels do not interact with humans on an "Archangel to Individual" basis, but rather they mete out justice on a group level. Think of them as those who help us to balance our group karma to become aware of our true selves through spiritual growth, evolution, and reincarnation. Without the understanding of what is bad in our collective behavior or thoughts, we would not have the desire to work toward the good aspects. We would sit stagnant, never trying to reach for happiness, love, light, peace, and prosperity because we wouldn't understand the hell WE created.

The Gabriels

The Gabriels call us at Death's Door. How many deaths do we truly experience in our lives? I am not talking just about the death of the physical body, for ourselves or another living being, but one of many situations or endings that can happen in our lives. Loss of jobs, relationships, or homes are all death experiences because there is an ending. Therefore, look at the Gabriels as those who help us bring about the ending of situations that no longer serve us.

The Seraphim

Humans are co-creators of the Earth. We are from the order of angels called the Seraphim. We are the "fallen angels." However, not all of us fell from this order. Those of us who did fall did so because we believed Lucifer and thought ourselves separate from the God-Source. This belief continues to this day, forming our thoughts and lives accordingly. Instead of recognizing we are creating our lives through our choices, it is the human tendency to look to others for guidance and help with making decisions. Truth is found without the negative aspects of ego. The negative aspect of ego created our fall from grace. Think of ego as an acronym for Edging God-Source Out. Ego is not necessarily a bad thing. When used correctly, our egos can stimulate our growth spiritually. When used incorrectly, our egos take us down. This is a powerful lesson for us to stop, look, and listen to what is being said to us and for us to decide if it resonates as truth before we make any decisions.

When we resonated with Lucifer's truth, we left the Sea of Bliss but stopped when we came to the earth plane. When we incarnated into the physical body, the realization of who we were was wiped from our consciousness. We will continue to incarnate until we have balanced the karma we have created on this plane and come to the realization that it no longer serves our highest and best interest to be on this plane of existence.

Many group vibrations can bring the high vibrations within us down. Have you ever been in a group where someone started gossiping about another and it brought the entire group into conflict? Think of that as you think of Lucifer bringing us down. Take a breath and think about where this one action may be at play in your life today.

The Cherubim

The next "ripple" out is the Cherubim. The Cherubim are the angels who stayed in the Sea of Bliss in their entirety. Because they never left the Sea of Bliss, I am not sure that their position or responsibility is clearly understood or known to humanity at this time. Often the memories held by humankind lead us to truth from those memories. Looking at our concept of the Cherubim today, we think of them as the bearers of love, the cupids, if you will. Love, pure unadulterated love, unconditional love, is what we all seek in order to hold and experience the space of oneness. It is important we come into the oneness and not hold ourselves separate and apart from All That Is.

The Raphaels

The Raphaels hold the keys to the universal consciousness or mind. We often hear the phrase "universal consciousness." It's a term presented by Anaxagoras, a pre-Socratic philosopher of ancient Greece. Know that it is where you will find truth, the truth of creation, of life, of knowledge. Without the Raphaels guarding this knowledge, this truth, we could ill-use it to hold power over another for our own gain. When we talk of the knowledge contained within, it is not only knowledge of creation, karma, reincarnation, and the knowledge of spirit, we also must include the gifts of spirit, psychic and healing abilities. Because our consciousness is not yet fully balanced with our subconscious and superconscious (or the lower self-balanced with the higher self), we would most likely use the information of universal knowledge to make our lives and the lives of our loved ones on Earth better, never worrying about the impact on other people and their lives.

Do not forget ego holds the space when we are hurt or injured. If we held the keys to universal knowledge, it would offer the incredible opportunity for us to do harm to anyone we feel has harmed us.

There have been many entities that have attained the Christ consciousness. They have come back to the earth plane to help others to reach enlightenment and have failed. This caused them to regress. The biggest cause of regression is the negative use of ego.

Grim Reapers

Lastly comes the Grim Reapers, whose job it is to meet us as our physical bodies die. Can you imagine the face of the person who has experienced their most recent life as an atheist being greeted by a Grim Reaper? I can only imagine the person peeing his/her etheric self at the appearance of a Grim Reaper. Seriously though, the Grim Reaper should be viewed as our escort to the other side.

We have the escort of the Grim Reapers. Therefore, you might be thinking, "Why do we have ghosts? Why do some individuals stay earthbound?"

- Someone passed away suddenly by accident and either denied the existence of the Grim Reaper or did not "see" them.

- There was a fear of leaving the earth plane and our loved ones, thereby refusing to go with them.

- When many people pass at the same time, such as during the Holocaust, many of those people didn't realize they were about to die.

- Confusion is another important factor. A fast and/or violent death will often leave those people unaware of passing into spirit.

Free Will

Throughout this book, I talk about the two different types of expressions of Free Will. When I am capitalizing Free Will it is to express our ownership of the gift of Free Will. When I utilize small caps I am describing the action of using our Free Will. In this manner, I hope to bring clarity to the gift of Free Will.

Free Will is a part of our experience. I had a hard time with this concept in my days of Catholicism. I was taught the God-Source gave us Free Will. Then I was also told the God-Source already knew how I would use it but I still had Free Will. This is one of those instances I had serious doubts. If I have Free Will, then using free will wouldn't be made unless or until I exercised it. Then it was my Free Will exercised by my decision. Since then, I have looked at Free Will from many vantage points.

I Have Free Will:

- I make a decision. The decision is felt as a vibration. The vibration resonates outward from me before I take any action. Thoughts are faster than actions. The decision through thought is felt from my vibration throughout the universe. However, as a side note, thought must have intention behind it for it to be karmic, not just random thoughts, and having a thought is not necessarily the utilization of Free Will.

- My soul holds the recorded history of all my lives: every minute, every breath, every decision, every thought and every action. If I am a part of the God-Source, then it follows that I am the God-Source. Everything I have ever been is also a part of the God-Source. Well, then so is my Free Will, and that would be shared with the God-Source.

I will add that Free Will is a concept that I will continue to meditate upon. Why? Because I am in linear time and on the mortal plane of existence. I still have much to learn regarding this concept. We utilized free will when we left the Sea of Bliss. Because we are a part of what we term God, that makes us God – therefore, the God-Source knows itself even better and the God-Source is experiencing our lives simultaneously with us.

Another Aspect of Free Will

It is that one gift, Free Will, combined with ego, which caused the fall with some of us falling farther from the God-Source than others. Many Christian teachings say that we must earn God's Grace and refer to someone who is doing "sinful" things as being unworthy of obtaining the Grace of God. Please think of the fall from God as the moment when we left to experience all that God-Source created. We didn't fall from Grace. We utilized our free will and left in agreement with the God-Source to experience all that was created. Now, because we forgot the truth of who we are, we are working our way back through our lifetimes of experiences to return to the Sea of Bliss. Do not think of it as a one-shot deal of being in or worthy of God's Grace. We are a part of the God-Source, and It wants those missing parts back. In a sense, we are incomplete while we wander in this physical plane of existence.

INTEGRATION

Religion teaches the God-Source created the universe and, in turn, our world. This removes our responsibility as co-creators. It also denies us the ability to fully understand we are the creators of our lives and how best to create our lives so we may come into alignment with our truths. This removes our accountability for creating drama, which is the result of negative emotions expressed through ego. This refusal to be accountable allows us to become victims of our thoughts and to become victims of each other.

When Good happens, ego allows for the patting of oneself on the back for a job well done and receiving our rewards. Instead of looking for bigger and better jobs, cars, and houses to be considered half as good as our neighbors, we fail to understand that we could have whatever we want; so whatever we have that is bigger and better is to suit our lifestyle, not someone else's. It happens when we understand we consciously create our lives through our thoughts and/or decisions.

To explain further, because most of us were raised with the concept of heaven and hell, be good or be damned, most of us think we have to be good in order to have good happen. In turn, we also are taught that bad happens because we deserve it to happen. However, we need to understand bad happens because we worry about it happening, so much so that we actually create it. We need to understand that emotions, or how we feel about a person, place, or thing becomes the stimulus to create events in our lives.

This concept is evidenced in the understanding of the Golden Rule and Karma. The Golden Rule states, "Therefore all things whatsoever ye would that men should do unto you, do you also unto them: for this is the law and the prophets." Karma is the spiritual law of cause and effect, the basis of which is "what goes around, comes around." Both of these concepts are right. Both of these concepts have left out a very BIG piece of information. If you buy into the concept that you are being punished for some wrongdoing, then you will be. You have created the punishment through your thoughts, most often through any guilt you may be feeling. The same holds true when you look at being rewarded for good actions.

When people talk about "waking up," it means more and more that people are beginning to understand creation on a much deeper level. When we understand we are creating our own lives moment to moment, it lays accountability for what is happening in our lives on us. When we take responsibility for where we are today, we understand we are not reacting to the actions of others but are creating the situation for them to act as we know they will.

The light, or energy, that is our true selves vibrates at a frequency commensurate with our thoughts and actions. You are the major player in your life. The people who show up in your life are the supporting cast. From an energy level, you will draw people to you who will either encourage or disrupt your beliefs. They are "chosen" for the like frequency they hold in alignment with both you and your goals. All of it is predicated on what you and they are working through to progress spiritually. This is why it is important to keep our minds, bodies, and spirits in a positive light.

There is a difference between beliefs and knowing. What we believe can be changed in accordance with what we understand at the time we believe it. Beliefs also leave room for doubts. Truth is a knowing, not a belief. Our beliefs make up our reality in this dimension. Moving away from what you believe to be true and moving into what you know will help you create profound changes in your life.

If we <u>know</u> a thing to be true, it will be. If we <u>know</u> a thing is going to happen, it will. When we move into higher levels of consciousness, we know we are creating everything in our world. The people who are our supporting cast, the jobs we have, health, wealth, and lifestyles we live are all created by our truths and are expressed in collaboration with each other. They, too, are the creators of their worlds and are drawn to our vibrations to be supporting cast members in their lives.

Removing the Concept of Mirrors

Most of us have a tendency to associate with people who come from similar backgrounds, lifestyles, cultures, education, intellect, and spiritual understandings. There is a myriad of reasons we are in each other's worlds.

The idea that we are all mirrors of each other is a good belief. This belief starts us on the path of finding truth. When we look at the concept of mirroring each other, we understand that the other person is showing us a personality trait, reaction, or something for us to recognize so we can accept it within ourselves.

When my mother passed away, I was in a deep state of grief. A woman who worked in the same office complex as I did told her office mate I was filled with anger. I wasn't; it was just grief. Was I the mirror of her anger? Was her reaction a mirror to show me how my grief was being felt by others? I didn't feel as though I was angry, and knowing how I act when I'm angry, I can tell you I did not show her anger. How she, in her beliefs, interpreted my emotions of grief was for her to understand.

I know that what is in me is not necessarily what is in another person and vice versa. I know the people I am around hold similar vibrations and thoughts as I do at the time in my life that I associate with them. It stands to reason if they hold a similar vibration, then their actions/reactions are going to be similar.

The mirror belief works well for many people. It helps them to recognize their own behaviors. A person you know reacts to a situation in a similar way as you might. You watch the reaction and decide what this person may be experiencing, doing, thinking, etc., predicated on how the situation would have made you feel. Just like the woman who decided I was an angry person did. The truth is she judged me as being angry because something in my behavior triggered a sense of anger within her. In other words, my behavior she interpreted as angry because that's how she would act in the situation. It is either a mirror (if she chooses to look at it that way) or a judgment. Either way works in her story. Had she known my mother had just passed, she may have seen something different within me.

Knowing we are creating our lives with our thoughts allows us to choose. The choice can be positive or negative. Thoughts are the most powerful tool we have, be they love-based or fear-based. When we know the truth of who we are, light energy, co-creating with the God-Source, we can then create our lives the way we want to experience them.

Knowing Truth

To live in our world doesn't require us to know anything more than we already know. We can just let our lives happen. We are creating our lives right now, most often by default. We will continue our lives, accepting the ups and downs as they come. We will give birth and watch people die. We too will live and die. We will complain about the struggle to pay our bills and we will continue to fight for our beliefs.

Creating our lives requires a different set of skills. Instead of reacting to what we have created, we must accept responsibility and decide we know our lives will be different if we create them differently. Shifting our consciousness to come into the knowing that we are co-creating our lives with others is powerful. The only requirement is to let go of fear. Fear is the emotion that creates everything negative in our lives. Letting go takes practice. More than that, it takes diligence and the willingness to look at what you truly fear.

My biggest fear was losing one of my children. How long did I hold that fear? From the moment my daughter was diagnosed with a blood disease at the age of 2, before her brother was even a conscious thought. He incarnated to me four years after she was diagnosed, and 34 years after he was born, he died. I allowed the fear of losing one of my children to create an opportunity and he fulfilled that fear. I do not pretend to know what truths he received from his experience with me as his mother in this life. I do know through his death, I no longer hold that fear.

Through his death came a higher state of truth. I know my son is closer to me now than he ever could be while he was on the physical plane. I have a deeper connection to him now because I can communicate with him more clearly and without the human emotions/fears/judgments that get in the way. Remember, our experiences day to day in conjunction with ego often get in the way of our earthly connections.

CHAPTER TWO

INCARNATION AND REINCARNATION

Before we can understand how we incarnated to this earth plane and why we reincarnate, we must first understand our fall as angels and our responsibility in this fall. Then, and only then, can we understand karma in its true definition. The noun "incarnation" is derived from the Latin word *incarno*, which is derived from the prefix *in* and the word *carno,* which means flesh. Combine the words and you have *into flesh.*

The Experience

As I explained in Chapter 1, the God-Source (of which we are a part) became aware of itself and creation happened. Some of us while we were angels listened to Lucifer and thought ourselves separate from the God-Source, the first step in the creation of ego. This meant our vibrations were no longer in balance with the God-Source, so we had to leave the Sea of Bliss. This is referred to as the "Rebellion." It was the Rebellion that precipitated "The Fall." The angels who rebelled fell from the Sea of Bliss (fell from grace) and fell to their own plane of existence in accordance with the levels of their Rebellion.

The Formation of Ego

As Seraphim, we along with other groups of angels, fell when we mingled with the stardust, feeling it emotionally and becoming a part of it on the physical level. To experience the feeling of emotion demanded the Negative Forces enter the Vibration. The term "Vibration" in this instance refers to the entity or being the spirit or angel was possessing. To direct and manage the Negative Force, a Positive Force took over. This unbalanced the positive and negative forces, accenting one force while weakening the other, depending on which action was dominant at the time. In that manner, we "split" our true selves, creating two halves from the whole. The other half of our whole is our true soulmate. When this happened, we became more aware of our own creation and less aware of the God-Source. As we drifted farther away from the God-Source, we forgot our responsibility in helping with the flow of creation. Instead, we became more and more enamored with ourselves. This is where ego was formed.

The Start of the Human Experience

As angels, each star and each planet represented a temptation to us. As we came upon the Earth we were enthralled with the sea, the winds, the forests, and the flowers. We began mingling with these creations expressing ourselves through them.

We began to experiment through the anthropoid apes, influencing them to walk erect, teaching them to build fires, make tools, and live in communities with each other. We influenced their bodies to lose the majority of hair while, at the same time, influencing them to become more "refined" in order to become more the way we wanted them to be. We did not actually start incarnating at this time, but we did start "possessing" the apes. We would enter the bodies and push aside whatever "energy" was there so we could experience physical expression. We did not stop at just experiencing the physical form but also experienced the sun, the water, and the plants through the physical form. At this point, we were still aware of who and what we really were - angelic beings.

Incarnation

Incarnation started when we decided we wanted to experience physical existence from birth to death. Incarnating through birth locked us into physical bodies. We no longer were possessing other Beings' bodies. We had become owners of the form we were in. Entering into this low-vibrating physical form wiped all memory of our true angelic selves from our consciousness. It was this decision more than the Rebellion and subsequent fall which set our feet on the path of karma and reincarnation.

For us to return to the God-Source, we must become pure in thought and understand our true heritage in its entirety, which is our true selves as part of the God-Source. We must realize we are co-creators with each other and the God-Source. We do this through the agreement of incarnation and reincarnation. Upon incarnating, the veil begins to drop. By age 7, the veil has completely dropped and we forget our existence in the etheric.

As spirits, we choose, through the vibration sent out upon conception, the life we will experience in order to fulfill our karmic obligations. Everything is included in this vibration. The parents are chosen because of the vibrational influence of their karmic debt and our ability to blend our karma with theirs. Because there is no perfect match, some of the parents' karma is accepted by the incoming spirit. Other factors include, but are not limited to, the location of birth (this comes in handy when understanding your astrological chart more fully), height, weight, skin color, and personality traits. Going one step further, as we know, within the construct of our DNA are possibilities of manifesting illnesses. This, too, is included because illness, both mental and physical, is a means of paying karma. A good book to read on the subject of karma is, *Many Mansions,* written by Gina Cerimenara. This book is a compilation of the transcripts of Edgar Cayce's life readings.

When we as spirits choose to incarnate, we create a destiny with the help and support of our spirit teachers and guide. The ultimate goal of one's destiny is to pay off karma, evolving to a higher consciousness in order to learn one's true heritage and earn one's way back to the Sea of Bliss.

Organized Religion and Reincarnation

This might be where the Catholic church took the understanding of the Rebellion and Fall of Angels into consideration when it established the ideas of Mortal Sin versus Venial Sin. Mortal Sin, thinking we were separate from the God-Source, versus Venial Sin, the mistakes we make that keep us from recognizing truth.

The Catholic church was the first fully autonomous Christian church on Earth. At one time, the teachings of the church included reincarnation. However, the people of that time started to become sloppy in how they handled their lives. Often choosing to "pay for it in the next life." This became a concept to justify their greed, envy, control, etc. In other words, the seven deadly "sins" were being enjoyed in the life they were living at the moment. The church chose to pull the information from the Bible (this was before the King James revision). There are parts of the Bible that still reference reincarnation. Furthermore, there is information regarding our "God Gifts" as well. Gifts such as clairvoyance, healing, and prophecy are some of the abilities we had and lost when we incarnated. (Please see the end of the book for a list of Biblical references.)

As stated earlier in this chapter, we split from our wholeness creating our soulmates. While we are on this Earth, in this life our counterparts are obligated to stay in spirit. The energetic draw between ourselves and our soulmates would create havoc energetically should we chance to meet on Earth. In fact, it is possible one would die upon meeting his/her soulmate. The Earth's energies might not be able to sustain such a meeting. Therefore, should, by chance, your soulmate HAVE to come here while you are here, every measure of precaution is required to ensure you will not meet.

This arrangement also has the added benefit of having your soulmate working in spirit to help you stay on track as well as working to raise the vibration for you both. The soulmate can be seen as our "voice of conscience" prior to doing something that will adversely affect us and our "guilty conscience" that speaks to us after we make mistakes.

The Five Bodies and Their Functions

Before beginning, I want to qualify something. There are people who teach about the mental, etheric, and ketheric template bodies as well as the causal body. The mental body is your consciousness and is not really a "body" per se. The etheric and ketheric templates are defined by some as layers of the auric field. The auric field and the causal body are not stand-alone bodies per se, but rather energy bodies coming from the physical form. This is useful if you are talking about healing or energy work. We are talking about Metaphysics and only the five bodies.

Light Body

Our first body is energy in the form of light. Light is our true form. This was when we were in the Sea of Bliss. The closer to the source of creation, God-Source, the higher in frequency is our light. The higher in frequency, the brighter the light; the brighter the light, the higher the vibration. Vibration refers to the oscillating movement (vibrating) of atoms and particles caused by energy. Frequency is measured in hertz units and is the rate of vibrations as the movement occurs.

When we raise our spiritual consciousness, the vibration (energy) of our physical form becomes higher in frequency. Why does this matter? The lower the vibration the more fear sets in. Fear creates negative emotions and actions.

Soul Body

As we left the Sea of Bliss, we took on the Soul surrounding our light to protect our true selves and to act as our "Report Card." I refer to it as a report card because it has every moment from every life, cumulatively speaking, recorded on it. Everything we do, everything we experience - good, bad, or indifferent are recorded on our souls. This record of what we do and experience is also in the Akasha, or God's memory. Do you remember hearing things like, "God knows EVERYTHING you do?" Well... this is why. NOTE: The Akasha is also referred to as the Hall of Memories or the Akashic Records. This record of spirit experiences is found on a plane, or a ray of vibrational energy, on what is called the 4th Resurrection. (More on the Resurrection in Chapter 3 - Karma).

Etheric Body

The etheric body gives form to and protects our souls and light bodies. This form usually keeps the form from the most current incarnation. As we realize, there is no time in the spiritual realm (etheric), so when we pass, the etheric body is a vibration. When our loved ones come to see us, they will be recognized by the last form the discarnate had to the person experiencing the visit. In other words, when my son makes his presence known to me in my life now while on Earth, I recognize his vibration. As I "feel" his vibration, the image of his physical appearance comes into my head. Mediums are impressed with the physical form of the entity coming through from the other side. This is so the sitter will recognize who is coming through from the other side.

Astral Body

When we incarnate, we take on two more bodies: the astral and the physical bodies. The astral body houses our light, the soul, and the etheric bodies. When we leave our physical bodies, consciously (astral projection) or unconsciously (during sleep), all the bodies are attached by the Silver Cord to the physical body so we don't get lost. This silver cord can stretch out to a "micro-inch." This can take us back into spirit or possibly to another planet. It is our safety cord. It has been said if you have your third eye open, you can look out over the city where you live and see your neighbors, friends, and loved ones hovering above their homes as they sleep, rejuvenating the bodies with prana (also called Chi, Qi, or Life Force). During sleep, we can also travel to the astral plane. This is where we work through our questions or problems, make plans for situations that are forthcoming, etc. The dream you have is from your astral experience. Think of the déjà vu experience of having already done what you are in the process of doing at that moment. When not dreaming, the rest of the time you spend sleeping is spent hovering above your home replenishing the prana.

When we die, our light or true form, the astral, etheric, soul bodies leave the physical body, but they are still attached to the physical form until the Silver Cord breaks. Once this cord breaks, the astral body and physical body stay behind as the etheric, soul, and light bodies transition back into the etheric. This is what many people refer to as heaven. This is why there was, and should be now, a three-day wake or sitting with the body before burial. If the body is cremated, the silver cord is burned up, meaning that it dissipates into nothingness. If the body is not cremated, the astral body can continue going through the actions of living until such a time as the astral body fades. The astral body can last a long time, at least until the physical body decomposes enough to let it go. It is the Astral Bodies that are seen doing the daily activities such as cooking, walking, or just being how they were while they lived here on the earth plane. Hauntings come from trapped spirits that didn't transition.

INTEGRATION

In the introduction, I told you this book was derived from classes I took at the church where I trained. These classes (now chapters) are meant as a foundation with which to build your truth. When I spoke of the Rebellion in the first chapter, it was the Rebellion of spirit or of the fallen angels to which I refer. This is a Christian concept, and I choose to place it in the chapters. I am sharing what I was taught. Please feel free to use this information as a bridge to gap the thought process from any teachings you may have had through organized religions and/ or metaphysics.

We are co-creators of the Universe. When Brahma breathed in, an expansion happened, and we became individual energy. We didn't actually "rebel," but because our vibration changed when we separated within the Sea of Bliss, it allowed us to become co-creators with the God-Source. We agreed to go forth and experience the cosmos and all that we could create. In this manner, we send our information back to the God-Source. Again, this is a level of Free Will.

As I have stated, we are not as strong as individual light as we are when our light is joined with the whole, or God-Source, which leaves us to understand that our God-Powers are not as strong as the God-Source. Humankind as individuals also co-create with each other. We create our lives by our thoughts, actions, and emotions to learn our lessons and progress. Our vibration will draw forth those who vibrate similarly, co-creating to learn lessons from us.

As we went out from the center of this energy (the Big Bang), our light started to dim. The further out we went, the dimmer our light became. As light beings, with our souls and our etheric bodies intact, we started having experiences as we traveled through the dimensions and the universe. Liken the dimensions to a multiverse, or maybe think of it as a level of awareness. Either way, we moved farther from the God-Source and started to experience life on the earth plane. We felt the elements and experienced the five senses. This is not to say we have never had experiences on other planets, in other galaxies, or in other dimensions; quite the contrary, we have. We did, however, decide to experience the birthing process, or we wouldn't be here. It was through this decision we lost our memories of our gifts of spirit and our light of truth. Understand that when we lost our memory of the truth of who we really are, it necessitated the action of reincarnation in order to regain the memories of truth. It is through the process of reincarnation that we create our lives to bring us back into alignment with truth. As we gain more truth, it brings us back into balance with the God-Source.

Incarnation/Reincarnation

At our first incarnation, the memories of our true selves were wiped from our consciousnesses. In subsequent incarnations, starting at about age 2, we started to lose the memories of being in the etheric. This happens through what we call the "dropping of the veil." The veil completely drops by the time we are 7. Most of us no longer remember being in the etheric. Some people may have some memories of being on the other side, in the etheric, but they are surreal. Others may have retained some of their God gifts such as psychic or mediumship skills, while still others retain memories of past incarnations.

Each incarnation is designed for us to progress to the level of understanding we had attained in other incarnations so we may rise above, as far as we are able, past that level of awareness. Although we are all as "old" as each other, what we did in our lives and the experiences we created helped to advance our spiritual knowledge to come into higher truths, and that is where each of us finds ourselves today. When we transition back into the etheric, we will take with us the sum total of the spiritual truths we have learned.

Two Experiences Found only on Earth

There are two things we experience on Earth that aren't found anywhere else: sex and time. Prior to incarnating through the birthing process, we possessed the anthropoid apes. We did this by pushing out their souls so we could inhabit their bodies. This is exactly like a demon possession talked about in churches. We possessed the anthropoid apes (Yeti, Big-Foot, etc.). We experienced sex as well. An element of emotion was expressed in the experience. Emotions create our beliefs, and our beliefs create our emotions. Women are the "negative polarity" (emotions), while men are the "positive polarity" (logic). To direct and manage the negative polarity, a positive polarity took over. This unbalanced the positive and negative polarities, accenting one polarity while weakening the other, depending on which action was dominant at the time. In that manner we "split" our true selves, creating two halves from the whole. Yin and Yang were out of balance.

When talking about polarity, women express the negative polarity; men express the positive polarity. The positive polarity moves outward, seeks, and embraces the logistics of life. The negative polarity is the emotion that moves inward. Remember, to experience emotion demanded the negative enter into the vibration. One is not superior to the other.

Soulmates

Many people love to lay claim to soulmates and twin flames. I am happy for you to do so if that is your understanding. I am not here to argue the right or wrongness of your understanding, only to offer mine instead. When we started incarnating, we "split" our true selves in half, creating two halves from the whole, the other half is your soulmate.

The point is, while you inhabit a physical body on this Earth, the person you lay claim to as your soulmate is a person with whom you have had many lives, and that is why you feel so comfortable with him/her. How many times have you thought (or said), he/she is my "soulmate," thinking you had a forever mate, then the relationship went south with both of you angry at the other? This is where the twin-flames concept was born.

Twin Flames

So much energy has been expended on this topic because it is a new concept. The concept of twin flames does not hold truth for me. My truth says it is just another term to describe a deep relationship with someone with whom you have had many lifetimes. When we incarnate, we have agreements with many people. The people who show up in our lives with whom we feel a deep connection to are people who have agreed to help us learn certain lessons. The lessons help us to grow spiritually or to bring about certain personality traits we have chosen to learn from.

The person we identify as the twin flame is so familiar that it seems like he/she is our other half. This concept may also be interchangeable with the idea of soulmates. As co-creators with each other, we bring in people to show us where we are broken. Often it seems as though they are our twin because their story is very close to our own that we resonate in harmony with them as we commiserate together.

A woman I know who works with twin flame explained to me that a twin flame is a person who is the other half of the spirit and that spirit split upon incarnating to have the twin flame experience. In other words, twin flames are each other's other half and the situation is designed to create a relationship to bring healing. Often these relationships are tumultuous and extreme and need a lot of work to be with each other. It is through the recognition of the self they meet that creates the healing by triggering the issues the other half needs to heal.

There are similarities in the concepts of twin flames and the Yin/Yang split when we first started incarnating. We have many people in our lives with whom we have instant rapport. We have shared many lifetimes with this person, and from the moment we meet there is an instantaneous connection. When we incarnate, we are constantly working at bringing in higher awareness and knowledge. The person whom people refer to as their twin flame is actually someone who agreed to make a connection on this plane in order to "trigger" the healing by bringing out the worst dysfunction of ourselves for us to see.

As a psychic/medium, I have had a few people come for readings and ask me when their twin flame will return. When I tell them it isn't going to be anytime soon, they refuse to acknowledge this. I can also tell you that from personal experience I have had a "Twin Flame" relationship experience as described by this Twin Flames section. This relationship was so intense, so connected, that to this day I miss our connection. I will also tell you that the connection was so deep, so intimate, and yet so dysfunctional, that I finally saw where I was broken and left the relationship. I have been healing, thanks to him, every day

CHAPTER 2 - INCARNATION AND REINCARNATION

since then. With that being said, no matter what you call it, no matter how you view it, I would encourage a person who has a twin flame who has left them not to wait until he/she returns but to continue the personal healing journey.

Linear Time

One of the aspects of the earth plane experience is time. Time, linear time, is a concept meant only for getting to work or for meeting each other for lunch, marking passage through the experience. Once you leave the Earth, there is no concept of time. No other animal or being on earth experiences time in the same manner we do. They sleep when they sleep, eat when they are hungry, and move about as they will. Time is one of the karmic tools for humans.

NOW vs Living in Linear Time

Understanding why you chose your current incarnation allows you the ability to take full advantage of creating your life in the moment NOW. Creating in the moment of NOW shapes your next moment. This will allow deeper integration with your human self and higher self.

To try to fully comprehend each moment of this or any other life is nonsensical. It just doesn't matter to our moment NOW. I am stressing the moment NOW so you begin to understand what happened last week, year, or another life doesn't have to be an albatross around your neck. Looking at your decisions – especially those decisions you seem to repeat - will give you an understanding of your beliefs. Once you understand your beliefs you can start finding your truth.

The only moment of the incarnation pertinent to you right NOW is the creation of the moment you are living now. You can make it pain-filled, dramatic, angry, racist, or phobic, or you can recognize the moment you are in as a beautiful expression of all that you are, past, present future. In this very moment, you are all that you want to be and you can also create that for your next moment.

When looking at this incarnation, know that all decisions that made up your experiences were good decisions if you learned from them. The experiences may have been expressed as bad or negative, but to fully let go of the fear that stops us from connecting to higher knowledge, we need to understand we chose this incarnation and we created everything from the first moment of incarnation to where we are reading this sentence now.

The one danger for all humanity is the "taking it personally" aspect. Each time we incarnate we do so for our spiritual growth. Everyone else incarnated for the same reason. The decisions someone else makes are to get them to their highest spiritual understanding, not yours. So when you hear the musical notes of "Somebody Done Me Wrong" song coming in to create anger, bitterness, or fear, remember they have perfect timing, too, and that you were vibrating at the same frequency and in agreement, creating the story in which you are now trying to victimize yourself.

Timing is everything. The timing is perfect. If you weren't capable of understanding when you found this book and you implement the information, which results in adding clarity to your life, you have experienced a moment of perfect timing. Timing in my life is in perfection, or I wouldn't be here writing this sentence for you to read.

The Five Bodies

First comes the light which is our true form. In Biblical thought, "God made man in his image." In Genesis 1:27, I quote, "So God created man in His own image; in the image of God, He created him; male and female he created them." I also offer from John, 1:18, "No one has ever seen God but the one and only Son, who is himself God and is in closest relationship with the Father, has made him known." The Bible was written and translated many times. I offer the idea that humans were largely uneducated at the time of the writings. When it was offered that God made man in his image, humans could only see themselves; therefore, they humanized the God-Source. The true self is light.

Our soul holds the record of all our experiences. Why, then, have a Hall of Memories, aka Akasha? It seems redundant. My training was that the Akasha is a place of existence in the Resurrection. What, then, is the Resurrection? It is a vibration or dimensional space. Another way to conceptualize the Resurrection is to think of it as a very large building with many floors and offices. Those offices are spaces to be filled with information. Think of the Akasha as being on the 4th Resurrection, or rather the fourth "floor" of the Resurrection in the etheric.

Many people will tell you they can read your Akashic Record. They are linking to your record through your soul body held within your physical body. Your soul body links to your Akashic Record. When we go deep into meditation, or maybe have a flashback, it is our soul to which we connect. My training has been that only those who have attained the Christ consciousness can access the Akasha for themselves and others. Jesus attained the Christ consciousness, and that is why he could heal others. He "saw" those who had brought the condition into balance for which they sought healing. If they hadn't, he couldn't have healed them, because to do so would have interfered with their destiny. Perhaps that is why so many who had attained the Christ consciousness lost it when they came back to help humanity. It was because their egos got in the way when they thought themselves superior. It could have been me or you who attained the Christ consciousness, but we will never know until we are able to access all our past lives in their entirety for ourselves.

The Etheric Body

Have you wondered why I use the term "Sea of Bliss"? It is because what we term "heaven" is actually the "etheric." This is why our etheric body is termed as such. It is the body that protects the soul and the true self while we are discarnate. This body gives a form to the energy of the soul and our light. The etheric body is a thought form. One of the uses of the form is to be recognizable to those still left on Earth, either by impressing the image of their physical form upon a medium to be recognizable to the sitter who has come for a reading or to appear to us if we are receptive enough to see.

For example, after my son Lance passed, I was given the opportunity to see Physical Medium David Thompson. A physical medium goes into a trance state, pulling the energy from sitters, (those in attendance) into his body. The energy is then transformed into ectoplasm. Ectoplasm is a thick, smoky, sticky substance that is the material from which spirit manifestations happen. Spirit will use this ectoplasm to slow their vibration down enough to speak in direct voice to those present, move things around the room, such as a trumpet, or form a body with which they can touch you. I was very fortunate my son came through the veil with aid of Mr. Thompson's spirit gift. I talked with my son and held his hands. Spirit was even able to manifest Lance's blue eyes for me to see.

When we transition back into spirit, we go to the etheric, and we vibrate at a higher rate. This isn't because we are automatically raised in consciousness but because the earth plane is a denser, lower vibration than the etheric. So, when you are wondering where we go, we go to a higher vibration with a faster frequency. The concept of going back to your "maker" or what I refer to as God-Source, is in truth what we are working toward. If you believe in reincarnation, then you understand we come back life after life to perfect our truths. Once we attain the Christ consciousness, we then move on to the next step (or level of teaching) back toward the Sea of Bliss.

The Astral Body

The astral body acts as a buffer between your etheric body and your physical form. We need this to help slow the vibration of the etheric body, the soul, and the light. When we leave our physical bodies, our astral bodies are tied to our physical form by the silver cord at the base of the skull. This allows us to go out of body and then come back to our physical bodies without getting lost. We can go into the astral, travel the Earth, and go to other planets or dimensions. Regardless of where we go, all we have to do is think of our bodies and our cords will "reel us in." One of the reasons to leave our physical forms is to re-energize our bodies with prana. Another reason is to work on our issues or problems. We do this in the astral plane. The astral plane is the third plane of Being. The earth plane is the first plane, or the material plane.

As noted in the foreword, many people will argue to death about the rightness of their thinking and the wrongness of others. I am offering an opinion or a thought with which to formulate your own truths, remembering we are not here to make others like ourselves. We are here to progress so we may come to the light of truth. In so doing, we make our lights brighter. The brighter our lights, the better for all. My truth is not necessarily your truth, because we have had different lives, with different experiences in those lives. Our decisions in those lives create our soul progression, depending on how or if we learn the lessons we have brought to ourselves. Truth never changes, but our ability to comprehend it does. Truth is a personal understanding.

CHAPTER THREE

KARMA

Karma is thought to be an Eastern philosophy that is defined by "actions seen as bringing upon oneself inevitable results, either good or bad, either in this life or in a reincarnation." (Dictionary. com). We can clarify this a step further by understanding what we are experiencing now may be the result of past incarnations.

Often the Western or biblical philosophy of the Golden Rule is defined as, "a rule of ethical conduct," usually phrased as, "Do unto others as you would have them do unto you" or, as in the Sermon on the Mount, "Whatsoever ye would that men do unto you, do you even so unto them." Mathew 7:12; Luke 6:31. (Dictionary.com)

The difference between the two is simple. Karma expresses itself as an action that can be immediate or a carry-over from one life into another, whereas the Golden Rule, coming from Biblical teachings, in which the concept of reincarnation is frowned upon, speaks more of immediate action. With karma the meaning is clear. You will experience an action that is the result of a preceding action. This can also include non-actions. It does not say, nor does it imply, you will experience the exact same action toward you that you expressed toward another. That concept is expressed in Deuteronomy as "Life shall go for Life, eye for eye and tooth for tooth." By definition, "an eye for eye" speaks to punishment in which the offender suffers what the victim has suffered." (Dictionary.com)

Karma started not with our Rebellion but with incarnation. When we decided to experience the physical body from birth to death, we became locked into the wheel of incarnation. Call it our "original sin." The more we incarnated, the more we got tangled in our karmic debts. Karma is the tool we use to bring the light of our true selves back to us. Truth never changes, but our understanding of it evolves as we work toward a higher understanding of truth. Plus, our spirit teachers help by revealing more truths as we progress. There are many concepts our minds cannot comprehend that will reveal even more truths. As we evolve, our vibration is raised and our light becomes brighter. The brighter our light, the more truth will be revealed and our understanding becomes greater. It is the spiral of knowledge we seek that will eventually take us back to the Sea of Bliss.

How Does Karma Work?

Most people see only the balance of karma as a payback for some deed of misbehavior they, or maybe another in their circle, expressed. Some people choose to view it as "God's sword of vengeance" or Divine Retribution. This is not very accurate but, understandably, humans tend to simplify. Furthermore, we mortals tend to view any upset in the smooth running of our lives as punishment.

Karma and the Akasha

Someone steals $100 from another person. This was an intentional theft. The action is immediately written onto both souls: the soul of the person doing the theft and the person who experienced the theft as the victim. This experience is then sent to the Akasha to be written in both people's "Book of Life" held in the Akasha. Within a nano-second, this theft is also sent/reported to the God-Source. The God-Source experiences the action immediately from the person inflicting the theft and the one that experienced the theft as the victim.

In the same nano-second, the experience of the theft by the victim is written on his/her soul, sent to the Akasha to be written in his/her

Book of Life and shared with the God-Source. Now both sides of the action have been felt by the God-Source.

The higher self of both parties, along with their spirit teachers, decide how to bring the debt into balance in the highest and best interest of both. Understand that the God-Source can see all that is written through the ages for all entities at any time. The God-Source experiences all our experiences and allows us Free Will to experience, learn and grow from the experiences.

God Gifts

As angelic forces or beings, we had God Gifts. We lost the memory of these gifts as we started incarnating. The veil between the worlds descends upon us by age 7. With more and more lifetimes experienced, more and more memory of the truth of who we are and what our capabilities are is lost. Our gifts include, but are not limited to, psychic abilities, healing, and prophecy. Consider our gifts as tools for spiritual unfoldment and progression.

Our God Gifts, when used correctly, raise our awareness of truth and our vibration becomes lighter. We begin to balance within and bring balance to our outer world. Unfortunately, those who use their gifts to harm, manipulate or take unfair advantage of another's circumstance for money, ego, or for any other reason that serves only them, run the risk of losing the right to those gifts. This brings with it the need to learn not to abuse power through lessons of karmic balancing. When we have truth within ourselves and use those same gifts for helping ourselves and others in a positive manner, our auras lighten and we seek the warmth of truth to continue growing our light. It is in this manner our karma will be given to us in a gentler, more productive, more helpful way. The God-Source's goal is for every spark of light - meaning us, every one of us - to reunite within the Sea of Bliss.

Karmic Balance

We do not always understand that every experience we have is paying off a karmic debt or creating one. Not all our karmic lessons are negative in nature. We reap what we sow. It is in our best interest to treat each other as fairly and as honestly as we possibly can, avoiding judgments of any kind, thereby not treating anyone or anything less than we would want to be treated.

We have complicated karma. Most people do not fully understand the true reason behind karma. It has become popular to blame karma. Lost my job...guess I must have fired my boss in a past life. Can't find a husband, must have been a bitch in a past life. Bob's wife cheated on him, he must have cheated on her in a past life. We may be right, but given our flawed mortal minds, we will be wrong more often than right. This "judging" ourselves or another should not be done. Regardless of right or wrong, karma can be incurred.

One of the most natural mistakes we make is trying to figure out karmic debt instead of understanding karma. In each section of this book, hopefully, we will come to a more thorough understanding of karma.

Judging

The concept of second-guessing or judging the rightness or wrongness of karma is one of the reasons for the phrase "judge not lest ye be judged." If we allow our higher selves and our spirit teachers to guide us and NEVER blame it on karma as we walk away, this action of accountability will help us to use karma correctly as a tool for higher awareness. We should look at our actions in every situation and hold ourselves accountable only for our portion. This and this alone will help us rise above karmic situations. By being accountable for our actions, we will recognize what we did and where we can change. When we fully understand our lessons, we are grateful for them. They help us learn and move forward. When we don't, we are doomed to repeat the process until we understand it fully. Again, the book *Many Mansions,* by Gina Cerminara, is quite possibly the best book I have read in understanding Karma.

Thoughts

Thoughts can be more powerful than actual action. The energy it takes to worry about something can consume us. Repetitive thoughts on problems or worrying can build in intensity to such a degree that it will create exactly what is feared. We need to learn not to negate ourselves and others through fear or any other negative thought. It is a true process of reaping what you sow. Our thoughts create our lives much like an author writes a book. Fortunately, and unfortunately, thoughts come before action and after the reaction.

Worry is the thought process of dwelling on the negative. Happiness is positive. There is much to the saying "Let go and let God." If we worry, we are not trusting ourselves to create lives for our highest and best interests. If we let go of worry and control, we trust our higher selves, our God-selves, to create the best for us. Find a way to take yourself out of worry. Listen to music you enjoy, read a book, meditate, and breathe.

After Our Agreement in the Use of Karma as a Tool

Once Karma was established and we became locked into the birth and rebirth cycle to pay (balance) that karma, the five root races were established. There were five Adams and five Eves. Each one represented one of the five races: Black, Brown, Red, Yellow, and White. Those of us who incarnated the first time, no matter which race we started with, lost our awareness of who we truly are. Having lost the memory of our true selves, we began to transgress upon others. This is what caused more imbalance and the need for more lifetimes to bring it all into balance. It is important for us to bring ourselves into balance so the light of truth burns brighter within us. As individuals, we are committed to reincarnating on Earth until we reach the level of enlightenment referred to as "The Christ consciousness."

Jesus' birth name was Immanuel (when he went back to the etheric, he took the name Immanuel again). It wasn't until he obtained Christ consciousness that he took the name Jesus. His destiny was to show us how to raise our consciousness. Through error, misunderstanding, and misinterpretations of the teachings he left, we deified him instead of following his example. We made him a deity. We then used his words to hold power over each other.

Parents Are Chosen

Plans are developed for a series of earth incarnations. The plans depend upon each individual, according to their karma and how much they continue to create. Every thought and every action of the physical body, along with its five senses and conscious mind, are in accord with the plan originally laid out for the spirit.

The parents establish a pattern or vibration according to their past lifetimes and what they need to accomplish. This sets up certain conditions of karma. An entity whose own karma blends with these conditions will be attracted by the opportunity presented. Since the pattern will not be exactly his/her own, the entity must consider taking on some of the karma of the parents in order to use the opportunity. This concerns environment, companionship with the parents, any siblings, as well as physical characteristics, location of birth, and even the day of birth. The entity must also be concerned with other situations in history, former association with the parents, the incarnations of entities it wishes to be with, and any other issues with whom it has problems to work through.

The parents are impressed with the name of the child. The child has three choices of names and then chooses the one it feels is correct for its path. The child's name and date of birth contain the right vibrations needed for the child's journey through life. The spirit guide and the spirit teachers are selected long before the actual physical birth to help the entity create its destiny. These spirit helpers are often referred to as "Guardian Angels."

The Spirit may occupy the body as early as six months before birth, sometimes at conception, as East Indians believe, or as late as two years after birth. The incarnating spirit can also hover over the body until birth, deciding whether or not to occupy it. Once the decision is made and occupation is completed (at age 2), the veil begins to drop between the new personality and the spirit, and the earthly record of the child begins. As soon as the occupation by the spirit occurs, the pattern of the spirit begins to work its way through the body, and the child's personality begins to develop.

Awareness of sexual identity is retained between lives but can only be expressed on Earth with incarnations. This is the only planet where we express the sex act and incarnate as we do as male or female. Remember, one of the reasons our true self split was to experience emotions. Adam and Eve, as is biblically referred to (symbolic for all mankind), were the ideal companions for the three-dimensional life on Earth to fulfill the physical, mental, and spiritual aspects. The Adams, who are the first males of each race, opened the door to incarnation and felt responsible for bringing the other fallen angels onto the Earth. They have vowed not to return to the Sea of Bliss until all of mankind is ready to return and incarnation is no more.

Death and the Next Incarnation

Many people have heard of the etheric and astral planes but don't quite understand the difference and use them interchangeably. Let's clarify:

- **Sea of Bliss** - Where creation happened and we came into consciousness with our True Source/Creator/God-Source/God.

- **Etheric** - What people term Heaven, Paradise, or Shamayim, is the plane of existence where we go when we pass from this life. Our spirit resides here when not in the mortal body.

- **Astral** - Where we go to work out our problems, get clear, and regenerate while sleeping.

- **Resurrection** – A dimensional space, or a vibration referred to within the etheric. When we die or are discarnate, where we exist in the Resurrection is predicated on our level of consciousness. For example, if a person holds a low vibration here on Earth and becomes filled with fear or anger and expresses it through animalistic behavior, they may be on the first level in the resurrection. Those who hold themselves as masters or superior spiritually may only be on the second level as their egos are driving their world. Most religions (if not all) have levels of "heaven" or, rather, the resurrection.

Our goal for each life is to meet the highest level of understanding we have attained cumulatively in our past lives and then progress beyond that. When we die, we do not go before the judgment of a deity. Instead, we judge ourselves through the "higher self." The higher self is connected to our superconscious and holds the accumulation of all knowledge and the level of awareness we have earned thus far. Prior to dying, we are to accomplish the following:

- Love totally, completely, unconditionally, if even for a moment.

- Be loved totally, completely, unconditionally, if even for a moment.

- Complete what we predestined to accomplish in this life to the best of our ability.

When we die, after the silver cord is broken, we go to a place referred to as the Sleep State. Just like the Akasha, it, too, is a dimension and vibration in the etheric. Just like when we are born on Earth, our tiny bodies have gone through an exhausting experience, and so does our spirit when we die. We need "time" to adjust. So, like a newborn, we sleep until we adjust. Some entities don't need as long as others to adjust. The sleep state is located on the 4th Resurrection along with the Akashic Records or God's Memory Bank.

To understand the levels of resurrection, also known as the etheric or heaven, think of a grid. Level one is at the bottom and each level goes upward from there. Think of the levels as a grade in elementary school. In school, there are certain lessons to be learned to pass to the next grade. As we pass each grade, each of those lessons contributes more light to our true selves. For example, two spirits incarnate to Earth. Both might have started this life on the same level, grade 2, level 2. When they pass from this life and are back in the etheric, a lesson that one spirit learned might pass them to grade 2, level 3, while the other spirit remains in grade 2, level 2, because that spirit didn't learn their lesson. We ascend through levels as our vibrations rise, just as we can descend through levels if we digress.

If the concept of the school grid is difficult, think of a beam of light from a flashlight. The light is strong and more intense close to the God-Source, and as it shines outward it becomes larger with the light particles being more dispersed, making it appear dimmer. We go to the portion of the beam of light that is closest to our vibration.

While in spirit we work with others, raising our level of awareness. It may be at this time our soulmate chooses to take a turn at incarnating. We, as soulmates, work diligently to help each other. If I fail and slide down in vibration, I take my soulmate with me as I go. So, as I stumble around down here, my soulmate works their hardest trying to help me by keeping the vibration high enough so that I don't slide down... or when I do, my soulmate is working in the etheric to help pick me up.

INTEGRATION

Karma is our greatest tool for spiritual enlightenment. Our karmic debt is a record of all our actions/activities, both good and bad, that we work to bring into balance so we may progress. Notice I said "work to bring into balance." **<u>Karma is not payback</u>**. A way to look at it is as an opportunity to see where we may be creating negative experiences in our lives.

We choose our parents. This choice is figured into our destiny path for our in-coming lives. We have to take on a bit of their karma and blend it with ours. This could be in the arena of intelligence, health, height, weight, etc. We tend to reincarnate with those families we have already shared lives with. This is because we have a karmic debt with them. It also follows that we have been our ancestors and are coming in to balance out those ancestorial lives with others of the same lineage that hold the same vibration or offer us a path to walk a destiny for higher progression.

Our choice to incarnate to our parents also offered us the ability to create our personality as expressed in this life. Everything about you was created by you to create for yourself the experiences you decided to have to balance your karmic debt. Our personality is one way we express ourselves throughout our experiences. It is also one of the ways we consciously create our lessons.

People react to us with the first visual they have of us. A person can be drop-dead gorgeous and someone will react to them negatively. Negativity can lower self-esteem, or it can be shrugged off as immaterial. How people act toward you is only important if you think it is. What is more important is how you act toward others.

If we choose parents who are well educated, the probability is high that we too will become educated. If we choose parents with addiction issues, the probability is high we will have many experiences with addictions, either being an addict or addicted to the addict. When we choose to incarnate, we plan our destiny according to the possibilities offered in bringing our karmic debt into balance.

It is a balance of both positive and negative karma that we are working on. Having too much negative debt can lead someone to experience fear and anger. Having too much positivity can play to conceit, greed, and control issues. Either way, ego is out of balance.

Think back to Chapters 1 and 2. I reiterate this because it is valid in each chapter, and it speaks to the need for a deep, very clear understanding that if we are to progress from one step to the next, our true selves must understand the need:

> "To experience the act of emotion demanded the negative polarity to enter the vibration. To direct and manage the negative polarity, a positive polarity took over. This created an imbalance between the positive and negative polarities, accenting one polarity while weakening the other, depending on which action was dominant at the time. In that manner, we 'split' our true selves, creating two halves from the whole."

The ability to balance karma is in the way we create our lives despite, and in some cases because of our choice of parents. This holds true for people who were adopted and even those stolen from their birth parents.

To understand karmic debt, look at what is repetitive in your world. Once you see the patterns, you will see what beliefs about yourself you have created. Once you become accountable for those beliefs from which you operate, you can make changes to balance those thoughts with truth.

How we choose to act through our lives creates drama or lack thereof. You are driving a car. Someone passes you on the left, cuts you off, and slams on their brakes. Does this irritate you? Probably. However maybe you held a fear belief that someone was going to pass you, cut you off, and slam on their brakes, so they did. If you know that doing that to someone else would be irritating to them, why would you do it? What do you think you would have to create to learn not to cut someone off in traffic: A car accident? A road rage incident? How about having been cut off in traffic, you learned that wasn't nice and decided to create a life where you no longer cut people off. We learn our lessons by recognizing them and holding ourselves accountable.

Once we have learned our lesson from the experience, we don't have to "pay back" the person who shared the experience. They will draw to themselves another with whom they will create their own experiences from which to learn. We don't have to worry about being someone's tool for their learning. Doing so might get us back in the quagmire.

Letting go of fear and judgment allows us to free ourselves from the outcome. It takes up too much of our time and too much of our good energy waiting for someone to suffer the ramifications of their own actions. Once you accept your lesson and move through it, your vibration is higher, and you will draw to you people who also hold a similar frequency. In that way, together you may create more learning opportunities.

We engage in thoughts of revenge when we replay a scenario over and over again. We create stress within our bodies, minds, and spirits. An imbalance in one area will also throw the other two areas out of sync. If your mind gets depressed, it does nothing whatsoever in helping the spiritual experience. Furthermore, when we create our lives through stress, we open the door to disease.

Global Karma

We not only have our personal karma to work with but as we create our lives through our higher knowing, our knowing becomes a part of the collective consciousness. The collective consciousness is an accumulation of all human thoughts. Therefore, some of us may have our knowing while others have their beliefs. The levels of understanding of truth vary from person to person.

At the time of this writing one of the most astounding leaders of the Civil Rights Movement, John Lewis, transitioned. In this incarnation, he experienced violence at the hands of others. In the 1960s when he and others joined with Martin Luther King, Jr., it brought civil rights to the consciousness of humankind. He had to stand in his knowing that he was equal. He was beaten for his truth. Being beaten didn't make his equality any less true. What it did do was open the door for that truth to become global. It's not that this truth wasn't resounding through many people for many decades prior to the 1960s, it just took a very long time for the collective consciousness to get behind the energy. Now, more and more people place their thoughts on equality for all within the collective consciousness. This allows the light to burn brighter for those who are still lagging behind. This brighter light will one day consume everyone's personal consciousness and we will see each other as equals. It has taken many years and the power of others in their knowing to provide the vibration necessary for the concept of equality to progress as far as it has.

As the collective consciousness globally begins to lose the fear of people, their culture, their color, their gender, their gender identity, financial status, etc., we will eventually come to the state of being called Universal Love. This unconditional love is found in the heart chakra. Understanding unconditional love means, there is not one thing that is loved greater than another thing. When it comes to humanity, as we learn to love unconditionally, we will have no judgment or fear of another or their life. You can see this battle come into this higher state of consciousness today as we witness people's fear-based decisions and opinions.

When someone holds fear within, their vibration is lower and their light is dimmer. You can see it manifest in them through the anger they display. We all experience anger. We are here to have human experiences, and emotions are a huge part of those experiences. The knowing of anger passes through us and is only a momentary experience. The danger comes when we hold that anger to intimidate and bring others into fear. Religion is the biggest culprit of fear creation. The fears were meant to control, subjugate, and manipulate people into the same way of thinking as that of the leaders of these churches. In this manner, they can feed their egos and get paid for it at the same time. **Fear is your biggest creator of karma.**

Chapter Four

JUDGMENT

To more fully understand karma, we look at judgment. Judgment is the taking of an opinion and making it a fact within our lives. Judgment is not necessarily based on scientific theory or fact but rather on emotions. For example, we are all standing in a circle. There are two people, a man and a woman, standing in the middle. They have an exchange of words and an object is passed from one to another. If I were standing in the position of looking at them, seeing the sides of their bodies with them looking face to face, I might see the physical exchange and think it was an exchange of something like money or even a piece of gum, depending on what it is I am thinking about at the time. If I were looking at the back of one of them, I might not see the exchange but may overhear some of the verbal discussion. From what I overheard, I would then come to a conclusion about the interaction. This is where judgment fails miserably. There are only two people who truly know what happened between the two of them. Therefore, to judge the circumstances or make an opinion based upon what you saw and turned into a fact using incomplete data is often where we make our mistakes when dealing with others. I should mention here that witnessing the interaction between two people is only a perception. Furthermore, each one of them has their own perception of what transpired between them.

Good Judgment

If we use our intuition to make a decision for ourselves and our own lives, we could probably cut the drama in our lives down quite a bit. And, yes, we also have to use good judgment when it comes to those decisions. However, if you are truly interested in using good judgment, talking it over with the others involved can lead to a better understanding of that which is in the highest and best interest of all concerned. You can also ask for guidance from your spirit teachers to show you what is in EVERYONE'S highest and best interest.

Bad Judgment

Bad judgment is best described as using our emotional fears to make a decision about what we or another should or shouldn't be doing. Remember the circle and the two people in the circle? If a woman has just been mugged, sees the exchange as described in the first paragraph of this chapter, then she might think the man is threatening the woman. She doesn't know this as an absolute fact, but she is guided to her decision based on her emotional fear. This can lead to a breakdown in trust and a situation out of control. Should she call the police, or is it just her level of fear that she has allowed to envelop her? By embracing her fear as truth, she may create another situation in which she is mugged or assaulted. Not only has she misjudged the interaction in front of her, but she has also allowed that misjudgment to give power to her fears, creating another negative situation for herself as well. Let me say here, that this is not about pointing a finger at someone to say it is their own fault if they are involved in violence. This is one of those negative experiences we have where we can change our circumstances by changing our energy around it and growing from it. Do not judge or try to manipulate this energy into some form of judgment.

When we form an opinion, then turn it into fact for any situation in another's life, we are misusing judgment. If we pay strict attention to our own lives, making sure we are following a truth path, we won't have the time nor the interest in another's life. Our own lives and vibrations would be rising higher and bringing in more enjoyable experiences for ourselves.

It is fine to give an opinion when it is solicited, but it is not good for our own lives to partake in the judgment of another. We do not know what a person's past life experience is, nor do we know what he/she has come to deal with for their own destiny in this life. Therefore, it behooves us to just breathe, meditate, and work toward our own progress.

It is easier for us to slide down into drama and negativity than it is to rise above it and hold our vibrations higher. Inspirational speakers are given accolades when they speak of how they have turned their lives around. As you listen to them, they tell you how you can do it too. They make recordings, write books and proselytize, giving you strategies that worked for them. We would buy very few of their books if they said it was extremely hard to rise above their drama and they were still struggling. The truth of the matter is you can make it easy or hard. Your choice is simple. Judge only yourself and your actions, leaving others out of it. Allow yourself to be guided intuitively or sit in the drama, slugging it out, judging others on their path as you sit in your own stink.

Karma versus Mortal Law and Judgment

To bring about stability in what otherwise could be chaos, mortal man created laws by which we have all agreed to live. We knew we were going to incarnate into these mortal laws. These laws are based upon our current level of awareness and the thoughts of the collective mind on Earth. The creation or amending of laws is an ongoing process. We grow intellectually, then we amend our laws accordingly. For example, in America when voting first became a right, only white men were allowed to vote. It wasn't until 1870 with the ratification of the 15th Amendment extending voting rights to all men (although for people of color, exercising it became more than a challenge). In 1920 white women were given the vote. In 1924 the Snyder Act gave Native Americans the right and, finally, the 1965, the Voting Rights Act made it possible for black women and Latinos to vote. This is a great example of how our shift in consciousness works.

The biggest problem with mortal laws is that mortal humans write them. We choose that which we feel is in our highest and best interest and our country's highest and best interest, then we vote on it. We should all remember that while we see our opinions as the highest and best interest for the country, our fellow beings see their opinions the same way. It is through their life experiences and their levels of consciousness that they make decisions on how they will vote. It doesn't mean yours is right and theirs is wrong. It just means that, cumulatively speaking, we base our decisions on our experiences. With social pressure and the news media, we are inundated with opinions. Gandhi said, "If we could change ourselves, the tendencies in the world would also change." He was/is absolutely correct. Focus on yourself and leave everyone else out of it. In other words, raising your vibration helps to bring up another's. .

Judgment Based On Societal Standards

No one likes a thief. What constitutes theft? The following are some examples of behavior patterns. Read through, pick the reaction to the statement that more closely aligns with you, and then you will be able to come into a clearer understanding of yourself and how your judgment creates your behavior.

The person in front of you drops a dollar on the ground. Would you...
1) Pick it up, put it in your pocket
2) Pick it up and give it back
3) Leave it, it isn't your problem anyway

The person in front of you is wearing a mink coat. They drop a dollar on the ground. Would you....
1) Pick it up, put it in your pocket
2) Pick it up and give it back
3) Leave it, it isn't your problem anyway

The person in front of you is homeless. They drop a dollar on the ground. Would you...
1) Pick it up, put it in your pocket
2) Pick it up and give it back
3) Leave it, it isn't your problem anyway

Judgment versus Justification

How do we know if we are using good judgment or just justifying our actions/decisions? This is where the self comes in. Johari's Window is a technique developed by two psychologists, Joseph Luft and Harrington Ingham.

First Window

Open/Free Area. The part of ourselves we and everyone else sees. This is the very basic surface of who we are. We are clean or not. We are tall or not. We are thin or not. It is the very basic level of who we are seen to be. Our skin color, our accent, our hair color, our clothing. It is the way we present to the world in a manner in which we would like to be perceived. If education is something you value, then you will present yourself as educated as you can possibly be, justifying that education is just as high a commodity as intellect. A plumber can be as intelligent as someone with a Ph.D.; they just don't have the certifications to "prove" it.

Second Window

The Blind Spot. This is the part of us that others see but of which we are unaware. We may think we are kind and compassionate, but in another's truth our actions can be seen as controlling, co-dependent or those of a martyr. In a more positive light, we may be seen as being more insightful and wiser than we think we are, thereby not utilizing our best assets for the greater good of others and ourselves. If we are lucky, we have friends who will gently share their views of us, both the positive and the negative aspects. If we truly look into our blind spots and work with them, we can shrink this area, creating a bigger, more open area in the combination of the first and second windows.

There is a saying, "Beware what you see in another, for it is within you." I am more inclined to say that it is often found within you. If you are seeing something, regardless if it is positive or negative, it is an opportunity to look within. You can also rephrase and say, "What another sees in you is not necessarily within, but something about you is triggering it within them." Our blind spots are about ourselves and are forever changing. You can use another's reaction to your words or actions to see within more clearly. Just make sure you stay away from justifying your actions.

Third Window

Hidden Area. This is where your deepest thoughts, emotions, and actions reside. It is a place for you and you only. Everything in this window is known only to the individual. This is where we keep our secrets and our fears, our wants that we are not yet willing to share with another. Why is that so? Why do we feel wanting to have something is shameful or that our fears are to be held within? It is because we are afraid that what we hold in this window can make us vulnerable or that we are unworthy. It could be a carryover from a past life when we needed to work on attaining whatever it was. Remember, there is nothing so bad, so shameful of what we hold inside that makes us unlovable to everyone. There is always someone who loves the worst of the worst offenders. There is nothing we want to have or to achieve that we need to avoid attaining. All of us have good within, therefore we are worthy. If we mishandled something in a past life, we should be working on manifesting it in this life. We may not get it. It may not be our destiny, but we should always strive for what we want. It will help us manifest it in the future.

Fourth Window

Unknown Area. This area is defined as that which our consciousness doesn't even know about ourselves. Therein lies our unrealized potentials. This could be where access to the super consciousness resides. Some examples in this area are:

- An ability that hasn't had an opportunity to manifest: intuition, artistic talent, music, math or science abilities.

- A fear unrealized. If you have never seen a spider, how do you know if you truly have a fear of one?

- An illness not yet known. Cancer, diabetes, and schizophrenia are examples of illnesses that may lay dormant until triggered.

- Conditioned behaviors from childhood such as anger manifesting later as aggression.

It is called the unknown area for a reason. Through meditation, we may be able to gain access to the information, thereby recognizing potentials we could manifest to create balance, spiritual growth, and understanding.

If we utilize these windows to grow properly to take a good, honest look within, we will be able to do away with justification. We wouldn't be making excuses for where we find ourselves today. Justifying is a great way to refrain from being accountable.

INTEGRATION

Judgment in today's world is a flame to a fire. We work diligently at judging our rights, wrongs, and the ways of others. What would happen if we just stopped? What if we quit seeking answers to situations that have passed? Why do we form judgments anyway? We judge because we seek reasons. This is what the left side, the logical brain, does for us. Look at the animal world. See how truly peaceful it is? The animals don't seek power; they seek food. There is always something more powerful than them, but they don't live in fear throughout their day.

What is the point of judging right from wrong? We know right from wrong. Why judge it? We know stealing is wrong. If it isn't yours, don't touch it. Why do we judge anyway? For the reasons of greed, envy, money, or pleasure. Any of the seven deadly sins can be placed here as the excuse people use to bring judgment on ourselves and others. Stealing goes against our higher consciousness. We can all manifest abundance. We can link into the abundant flow of the positive, but not when we are causing negativity. Judging someone's actions or even our own is a negative act. If you are judging yourself, become accountable and make amends. We should be correcting our actions consciously before our higher self creates a way to bring balance through karmic lessons. If you are judging another, you will create the opportunity to experience the reason why they did what they did to learn not to judge them for their actions.

Understanding the concept of creating one's own life to grow spiritually is why we bring situations to us. A pregnancy in which an abortion is considered and/or undergone may be right for one person but not for another is an example. Withholding someone's access to a free will decision goes against our rights as co-creators.

This is often how judgment works against us. It creates fear, envy, low self-esteem, and division. It creates everything that is negative. Fear comes before all negative emotions and actions, and love comes before positive emotions. When we get so fixated on judging, we forget to simply experience the moments. When we forget those moments, we become focused on the negative. This lowers our vibrations. Then we begin to worry others will judge us, and we worry they won't like us. Worry is a fear-based emotion. It is a repetitive thought that runs through our brains. The more we worry about a given situation, the more energy builds and brings it forward.

Here are some insights about fear. These are all sayings that have come my way throughout the years. Nick Vujicic gave us the acronym for F.E.A.R., the second one, I believe, is a quote by Gordon-Michael Scallion from his book, *Notes From the Cosmos: A Futurist's Insight Into the World of Dream Prophecy and Intuition.*

- FEAR is an acronym for False Evidence Appearing Real

- What you resist, persists. What you fear, you draw near. What you emanate you create.

Mortal law is a human experience. We live by laws we create to grow as a society. As we have experienced in our society, the laws are often used against us. We have a Supreme Court that researches the laws, the constitution, and all the amendments to uphold a law or strike it down. As noted previously, laws are written predicated on the information at the time of the law being written and where the collective consciousness is at the time.

Change happens when the status quo moves into higher awareness. As the vibration of higher consciousness lifts the consciousness of our mortal mind, our vibration and frequency rise. What was once the status quo may no longer be applicable. As we grow in consciousness, we amend the laws accordingly. We all know slavery is an abomination, and slavery has been going on in the world for thousands of years. We know it still exists today. The last I read, there were 12 million people without a country of origin. They were taken as children and forced into the sex trade industry. They are often held (or murdered and disposed of) long after their usefulness in the trade has dissipated. We find them in many industries in America and across the globe today.

By the use of our intuition, and meditation practices, we begin to lose our desire to judge others. We seek higher guidance and when we realize we are in error, we self-correct. I didn't say self-condemnation, I said self-correct. This is about being accountable and making changes as we grow in higher awareness. This isn't about wallowing in guilt. This is about understanding we have done something that isn't in our highest and best interest and correcting the behavior.

There are so many people who are "fighting the good fight." Each of us in our own way is using our judgment to create our experiences to progress in the ways of spirit. That is all we can do. If we feel compelled, we can take up the political stance and ask our elected officials to govern our cities and states in a way to stop abominations like human trafficking, aka modern slavery. We can enlighten others about the plight of the slaves. In Canada, they have the "No More Stolen Sisters" campaign. There are a number of ways you can deal with this. One way is to connect to your intuition for answers.

GLOBAL AWAKENING

CHAPTER FIVE

CONSCIOUSNESS

This is the only chapter in which you will see me make a clear qualifying statement. There is a vast difference in what is meant by the use and function of the conscious mind, subconscious mind, and superconscious mind in metaphysical versus psychological functions. The psychological aspects and understanding are of the earth plane while the metaphysical is of the etheric or esoteric plane.

The mind is an instrument of awareness. Used correctly it is powerful and increases in its capacity the more it is used. The more it is used, the more it will continuously unfold into new potential. Instead of using your mind to "head talk" against apparently unsolvable problems, worry about what the next step should be, or what you should or shouldn't do tomorrow, try to form the habit of listening with your mind or seeing what you want in your mind's eye. Use it as an instrument of awareness. Let the cosmic consciousness fill your mind, thereby making your body, mind, and spirit an instrument of the God-Source. The cosmic consciousness is the divine oneness of consciousness in every being throughout the multiverse. Unity with the God-Source creates the ability to progress more in the ways of spirit.

Jesus taught that man can realize his oneness with the creative mind through conscious communication with the God-Source. Through this oneness, we can bring about peace, harmony, and wholeness. We do not know from moment to moment how our lives may change, nor do we know where or how the change may take place. It may be found in a moment, a book, a message, a person, or through whatever means that triggers your soul to open. Think of the limitless influence and harmony of your life when you open up to the love attained through the oneness with the God-Source.

When you can look at every man, woman, child, animal, vegetable, and mineral on the earth plane and see the God-Source within all, you will then develop a consciousness that never looks and judges anyone or anything. You will have the ability to see, feel, and love the God-Source within all.

The superconscious is that part of us that holds the truth of our creation, our exodus from the Sea of Bliss, our karmic agreements, and our level of consciousness as it unites us to the God-Source. The superconscious is our Godself. This is because we are a part of the God-Source, therefore we are God-Source. It is also our link to the higher self and other places/dimensions.

The subconscious holds memories or indications of past life experiences. It is between our superconscious and our conscious mind. It is here where we can, through meditation, connect to the realization and understanding of our gifts of spirit. It is also where we draw forth that which our conscious mind creates.

Conscious mind came into being when we incarnated. We lost our connection to our superconscious and only had limited access to our subconscious minds. From the first moment we incarnated, we lost the memories of our true selves, totally and completely. Each generation has to relearn the truth of our being. We utilize our conscious mind to hold our thoughts, deeds, and learned information, to create the experiences which bring in awareness and balance karma in this lifetime. It allows the logical and emotional bodies to co-exist. It holds the theories for which we use the sciences to gain more understanding of our physical world while, at the same time, bringing in thoughts and theories in philosophy. Many truths have become untruths, and many untruths have become doctrine/dogma.

Music, numbers, and geometry were developed and brought into the physical experience from the etheric to bring upliftment to our mortal existence. They are not just for our listening pleasure, counting money or items, or equations to build buildings. They also hold within the construct of truth.

Music has a vibration of its own. It brings to us concepts of joy and happiness, uplifting our spirits through the beat (drumming), words (song), harmony (balance), etc. The language of music can inspire our emotions to create positive and negative experiences.

Numbers brought an understanding of vibration and frequency. Math is the language of the universe. From the moment our children are aware enough to conceptualize numbers, we teach them to count. As soon as we see they can solve simple math equations, we teach our children to calculate. Once we began to understand math, we were able to find the frequencies. The names we were given, and the date, time, and location of our birth all hold numerical values. Numerology and astrology, when done correctly and on a personal basis versus an overall generality, give our individual selves an inkling of the abilities we can manifest in this life.

Geometry supplies the building blocks upon which cities are built, and, in turn, these cities provide shelter. However, what is referred to as Sacred Geometry is the utilization of universal patterns that create our entire Earth experience, from vegetation to sacred architecture. The basic belief is that through understanding Sacred Geometry and mathematical ratios, harmonies and proportion are found. When we find the harmonies and proportions in music, we begin to find the cosmology or the origins of the universe.

Theology and philosophy are ways to express ideas that were held within. The entirety of truth had been lost and theology and philosophy were the paths back to those truths. From theology came religion. Religion became a list of rules. These rules were designed to help us hang on to the truth of the Godself. Unfortunately, religion became a ritual of longing for truth instead. We all are on a different level of understanding. With religion came different ways to practice stemming from the differentiating truths. These different truths, touted as being the only way in which we find truth, became more misinformation due to interpretation. Philosophy, however, creates opinions of theory which then initiates the connection to our God-Source. As philosophy stepped forward through theory, it became the light at the end of the tunnel. Under the guise of philosophy, we have begun, once again, to share ideas and ideals. Through the expression of religion, we became dogmatic and tied to the rules. Philosophy also gives us the freedom to discuss possibilities without dogma.

As a result of each person's state of consciousness, and what they could accept, many different philosophies and theological opinions resulted over many, many centuries. These will eventually merge back into metaphysics (the science and study of all), which has always existed and predates all religions. Each entity will know they are a part of the God-Source and that they and the God-Source will be one again.

Humanity has lost all knowledge of the truth they once knew. We started believing only what we could see and prove through science in accordance with the conscious mind. The only tools we had left were positive and negative experiences, such as love versus suffering. It is through the utilization of these tools we will advance and our conscious minds will merge with our subconscious minds. When our spirits are no longer prisoners within our physical bodies and are as free within it as out (as with conscious astral projection), the earth cycle will be finished. When our Free Will is in harmony with the God-Source, we are then ready to ascend to the next levels.

INTEGRATION

Superconscious Mind

The superconscious can be viewed as a senior adult, an oracle, or priest/priestess if you will. This consciousness is untainted by the third-dimensional thought process of patriarchal, religious, or corporate control. When we incarnate, we hold within the truth of who we are as immortal, spiritual beings. It is the dogmatic approaches handed down from parent to child that make us forget who we are. We then begin to live in fear. It causes the superconscious mind to recede farther and farther away from us. Unless, of course, we decide to start breaking the patterns taught to us. Then the world starts to change.

It takes time and practice to access the superconscious. One of the reasons it takes so much effort is that our conscious minds get in the way. The mind tells us what we are going to experience instead of letting the experience happen. We have roadblocks of mistrust that were formed from years of programming. There are many reasons for the disconnect.

If we could just fling open the door to our current state of consciousness, would we be ready for that? Everything I am sharing with you through this book has come to me through study. It has taken me my entire life to get to where I am today. It wasn't just an immediate "BANG" and the knowledge was thrust into my head. There was training. With the training came an awakening. With more training came more truth. We already have the knowledge. All we have to do is meditate and be open to the information. We have to be willing to allow the truth to come in, then work with that truth to gain more truth.

There is a lot more truth about being here than we know. It is the Christ consciousness we seek to attain while on the earth plane. If we can let go of all our fears, doubts, and mistrust, we will be able to handle the truth of who we are. It isn't so much the truth of who we are as spiritual light. It is the truth of who we have been in various lives and what we have done. This is why we work at attaining the level of awareness we have accumulated in other lives so we rise above that.

This book is about awakening to higher levels of truth. We are here having a human experience and raising our conscious minds to the level where we can get the superconscious, subconscious, and conscious minds to create in unison in accordance with higher levels of truth. If we allow the knowledge found in the superconscious that holds the memories of the truth of other timelines, galactic experiences, etc., our experiences will be available to us. This is a key to opening the door to the possibilities of working with earth experiences.

Subconscious Mind

The subconscious is the aspect of ourselves best likened to that of a mature adult. Mature adults have made many errors throughout their lives. Sometimes we learn from those mistakes. Sometimes, due to conditioning as a child, we repeat them over and over again until we create a situation so difficult to get through that we promise ourselves never to do it again. An example of this is when we get into the same types of dysfunctional relationships with the same types of people, repeating the same types of actions until we reach a point where we understand the dysfunction is created by the ego and we let go of the need to be right or wrong.

Have you ever experienced or had a memory of who you were in another life, in another culture? This is where we start to build those repetitive patterns. As past lives touch in to show themselves to us, we start to understand what we have created in the past and how to heal within ourselves now. Through meditation we can access other lives that have influenced our path this lifetime. It is important to bring in healing for ourselves in this life because as we heal, we heal the generations above us and the generations below.

It is best not to use guided mediations solely. Learn to sit quietly with yourself. It truly is a wonderful experience. You will be shown and given answers to all of your questions. It's fine to use guided meditation once in a while, just don't make it a habit in which you become dependent upon it. Learning to quiet the mind will allow you the opportunity to ask questions, and in quiet solitude, your subconscious will help you gain access to your higher self to give you the answers.

Think of the subconscious as a buffer between the conscious mind and the superconscious mind. It holds valuable information. If we train, we will be able to access the information when needed. Our subconscious holds the programming from experiences we have had in this life and other lives. The information can help us to understand our karmic balances.

If we struggle with financial abundance in this life, there may have been many lives in which we lived in poverty. Poverty can become such a wound in our spiritual self that we keep re-creating poverty to move past it. The statements we might have heard in this life that can reinforce the poverty belief may have sounded something like, "you don't deserve," "you will never amount to anything," or "you are stupid." All of these types of negative statements can reinforce the fear of never having enough. Add an action currently happening in your life, such as a drought that makes food scarce, or a thief who may have robbed you, which will set up instances that reinforce the pattern in the consciousness which relays that information to the subconscious and superconscious minds. The conscious mind then starts to create scenarios so we experience more poverty. This will happen again and again until we consciously choose to create different lives.

When you leave the earth plane and go back into spirit, there is no linear time. Our lives are happening simultaneously, as odd as that may seem. Knowing lives are happening simultaneously, we are more open to accessing the necessary information and bringing it more readily into this moment. Think about it. If your subconscious can get you the information you need to heal a situation from the future you, why wouldn't you?

Conscious Mind

The conscious mind is like a mischievous child. A child thinks of having fun and playing games, and so does the conscious mind. Often we struggle with doubts and fears, imagining the worst-case scenarios popping up in our lives pertaining to the area in which we are thinking. We fear being sick, so much so that we actually open the door to illness. Maybe we fear being alone, so "unconsciously" through the conscious mind creates situations that reject someone before there has been a chance to state intentions.

Most people think negatively. This creates chaos and drama within our lives. Statements such as "I wouldn't put up with a boss like that" open the door where we soon find ourselves with a boss just like the one we thought we wouldn't tolerate. If you are asking why, then you have come to the understanding that it is something you need to deal with, something to heal within you, or you wouldn't have seen the boss as someone you don't want to deal with. Our negative minds and emotions have much more power than our positive ones.

Our conscious mind is busy during the day creating the next moment of our lives. It makes lists, drives the car, accesses possibilities, pays bills, loves our family – or not. It feeds the cat, walks the dog, makes judgments, gets angry, takes things personally, takes things for granted, forgives, replenishes our hearts, and generally does a million and one things. That is a lot. How much is really important? You're right… all of it. The greatest moments and the greatest ideas come when you use your conscious mind to consciously create a better tomorrow for yourself.

Doing this, surprisingly, takes very little effort. It is about resetting patterns. Each time you say something negative, then follow it up with something positive such as, "I love creating love." A friend of mine is famous for using the phrase "white light" when she comes across negative speech. I have a tendency to say, "I just love you." Although, admittedly, I don't say it often enough and foul language can spew forth in a hot-tempered moment.

It takes time, effort, and willingness to dedicate ourselves to bring in change for the positive. It is life-altering. Understanding the three separate minds allows our gifts to come forward. It also allows us to bring change to our world and our lives. If anything is going to change your world, it is coming into an understanding of the three consciousnesses and working with them.

CHAPTER SIX

CIVILIZATIONS

The last few chapters are heavy in cross-over information. It is very important we work through these next few chapters with an open mind. As we look into civilizations, I am reminded of an excellent book to read to more fully comprehend the various changes brought through these civilizations. You might want to consider reading Michael J. Roads' book *Into a Timeless Realm*.

We are used to thinking of a civilization as a way of life under a certain rule, such as the Roman Empire. In metaphysics we understand a civilization to be approximately 250,000 years (12 cycles of 12 ages) under the rule of one of the five root races. Consider a civilization as a time period through which major shifts and changes occur to bring humanity to higher consciousness. An example would be the Atlantean civilization. It is said that we are closer to the knowledge the Atlanteans had in science and metaphysics than ever before. In a civilization one race dominates. This is not saying the race is superior, but rather the work of that particular race is the dominant factor governing that age. Knowing this and understanding that through the approximately 250,000-year cycle of a civilization, the lives we experienced were expressed through all races, and more than once. In other words, each human has been black, brown, red, yellow, white, male, female, gay, straight, rich, poor, etc., in each civilization.

There is a difference between the term civilization and what is referred to as an Age. An Age is a time span, (approximately 2,100 years), ruled by an astrological sign. We have left the Piscean Age, and are now in the Aquarian Age. The Aquarian Age started in approximately 1962. The effects of the Piscean age have had to slowly dissipate. This happens as people step into the new vibration and mind shifts start to happen. The Piscean thought process has finally abated enough for the potentials of the Aquarian age to start showing.

As previously discussed, there are five root races, with five Adams and five Eves. We are aware of some of the original Adams but not the Eves. This is possibly due to the masculine (patriarchal) vibration dominant now.

CIVILIZATION	RACE	ADAM
Mu	Yellow	Buddha
Da	Brown	Jesus
Lemuria	Black	Muhammad
Atlantis	Red	
Ra	White	

I have left out the Adam of both the White and Red race because I do not have this information. Additionally, I have left out the names of the Eves as patriarchal religion has lost these names. We know little about some of the civilizations. As we go from one civilization to the next, we understand the teachings of those civilizations are along the same lines as what we are working with to evolve now, such as a spiritual state of consciousness in which we learn to live as a cohesive faction of spiritual enlightenment instead of a torn community of idealism.

Lemuria

Lemuria was in the area we now know as the Ring of Fire in the Pacific Ocean. Catalina Island was the highest mountain top in Lemuria.

The time of Lemuria was before Atlantis. The people were highly evolved and very connected spiritually. There has been much discussion in the scientific communities regarding whether this civilization existed. It did, and many people have memories of having lived in Lemuria. It is important to understand we have had lives in each of the known civilizations such as Lemuria, and we have also lived lives in other parts of the world at the same time Lemuria was dominant. This knowledge helps us understand our global lives today.

Atlantis

The Red Race ruled civilization during the time of Atlantis. Atlantis covered the Atlantic Ocean area, Iceland, Greenland, Bimini Islands, and South America. Today, our understanding of science, universal knowledge (also known as metaphysics), and the development of our spiritual gifts are as close to the knowledge of the Atlanteans as we have ever gotten.

Other than our current one, Atlantis is probably the civilization we know the most about. The scientific communities of Atlantis found ways of working with DNA and DNA combinations to create new species. This is probably one of the reasons why people are so against cloning and stem cell research. The Atlantean scientists learned to control the weather with crystals. They also learned how to perform lobotomies on their criminal factions. The book titled *Edgar Cayce on Atlantis* written by his son, Edgar Evans Cayce, tells of America being the penal colony for Atlantis.

Atlantis' scientific communities were at odds with the healing communities. The healers worked in temples with crystals, healing energy, and natural remedies such as herbs and foods to bring about healing of the physical body, which of course brings balance to the mind and spirit also. The scientific community had begun to experiment with the combining of animal DNA with Human DNA. This may be why pig insulin was found to be more aligned with humans than the insulin of monkeys or apes. The differing opinions on bringing about healing created division within Atlantis.

The scientific communities and the healing communities both believed in the concept of phenomena. This is to say they both recognized and worked with the energies of what we refer to as "gifts of spirit." For example, Atlanteans used the power of the mind to levitate stone and/or a hover ship (a large space ship sometimes referred to as a Valix) when moving the stones into place to build. These stones were cut by lasers with extreme precision.

As all Atlanteans had developed their spirit gifts and, because of ego, they used them against each other. Earthquakes started to happen when the conflict between science and spiritual communities began in earnest. There were crystals used in weather control to provide energy for heating and electricity, etc. These crystals were deliberately blown up resulting in the destruction of Atlantis. The Albuquerque, NM, area was one of the areas in which the power crystals blew up. This was approximately 12,000 years ago. This cataclysmic chain reaction is what is referred to in the Old Testament Book of Genesis as the story of Noah's Ark.

Da

It was when Da ruled that all five root races were here at the same time. From that time on and to this very day, all the root races were/are located in different parts of the world. Each root race has had the opportunity to rule, and in each case they failed due to corruption and socialistic type thinking. It is difficult to learn the lessons of the seven deadly sins such as greed and envy when the entire society is on equal footing. In the same thinking, we have abused the concepts of capitalism, which is why the cries for socialized medicine are so loud. There has to be a healthy balance.

In a socialistic society, the production, distribution, and exchange of goods and services are owned and/or regulated by the community as a whole. However, in remembering that we are here to bring forth truth for the spiritual progression of our higher selves through the balancing of karma, the socialistic principles are in direct conflict with the way we bring our lives into balance. This is because there are different levels of spiritual enlightenment in humankind. In some, the varying levels are expressed through the desire for power and control resulting in greed and corruption. While, in theory, it is nice to think we should all be able to thrive in a socialistic environment, we would ALL have to be of advanced spiritual knowledge, resulting in the willingness to share equally in both accountabilities and actuality.

There are many stories we have passed down from generation to generation, from culture to culture, and passed on to the next culture which speaks of these things. We find them all fascinating and interesting in the moment, but other than enjoying them, we don't know whether or not to believe them or consider that they hold value in our daily lives. This couldn't be further from the truth. We are so divided as a species on so many different levels, not just politically or religiously.

As previously stated, if we understand we all reincarnate, then we understand that during each civilization we have been a part of the dominant race and a part of the races which were dominated. We have chosen lives in which we experience being male or female, heterosexual or homosexual. We have lived to be old and infirm and have died young. As we have all realized, there is nothing the generations before us haven't already experienced. There is nothing new, just our reaction or response to it and what we learned from it for our spiritual progression.

There is always an energetic crossover when moving from one age to another. The Aquarian children started incarnating in the late 1940s and 50s. They had some karma left with the Piscean energy to be worked out. So, while the Aquarian Age started in 1962, the energy of the Piscean Age was still felt as recently as 2014.

The Christ Consciousness and the Age

Jesus is the Adam of the Brown Race. He attained the Christ consciousness during the early part of the Piscean Age. The Christ consciousness is the highest level we can attain on this plane of existence. A person who has attained the Christ consciousness has opened up all their gifts of spirit and has a higher level of spiritual understanding. Gifts such as bilocation and dematerialization are some examples of higher consciousness gifts. There have been people who have attained this level of spiritual understanding, but we do not deify them. Today people refer to higher levels of consciousness as attaining the fourth, fifth, and sixth dimensions, which is to say they have a higher state of consciousness than the average person.

Jesus' teachings still rule the teachings of Christianity today. He is known as the Healing Christ. If you read the New Testament, his teachings were about the healing of the mind, body, and spirit. Jesus also taught that in bringing about our own healing, we would then come to love one another. The teachings were originally nonjudgmental. However, after much editing and the reinventing of the Bible, it has become a book of judgment. Jesus did not teach that man ruled over women and children. This was yet another concept created through the reinterpretation of the scriptures that make up the more accepted Bibles of Christianity. The most popular Bible in use today is the King James Version, published in 1611. One of the oldest versions of the Bible in evidence today is found in the Vatican. It is known as the Codex Vaticanus and is from the fourth century.

Buddha taught we are to develop the brotherhood of man. The brotherhood of man (human) is the understanding that all are equal, and when the understanding of equality of all humans is attained, then the Golden Race will emerge. At that time Buddha will become the reigning Christ consciousness. We will no longer have the division of race separating us. There will be more about this in the chapter on Precepts.

Understandably, as we work toward the crossover between Jesus' teachings and those of Buddha, some people will have a difficult time making the shift to that level of consciousness. We have many political leaders at this time struggling with making their voices heard. We need to recognize these divisions. We need to hear their voices and make conscious decisions not to accept their fears and the values those fears bring to the forefront. Their words are a mirror of our own voices, showing us how very negative and divisive we sound within our own hearts and demonstrate through our own actions. Remember that we have a destiny. That destiny is to raise our consciousness high enough so we can merge it with our subconscious to reach our superconscious. We are all light, but we need to hear, see, and feel the dark so we decide through our own Free Will which way to express our human experiences lead to our spiritual growth.

We are standing on the verge of a new civilization and a new age. The Aquarian Age promises to be one of light and unconditional love.

This is a time when we are to create the Golden Race, meaning there will no longer be a separation of races by color. Even though we all hold the same DNA, our expression of our individual lives through our DNA is different. The eighth ray has been cast. (Again, more about this in the chapter on Precepts.) The vibration on the earth plane grows stronger, reaching higher. To bring this new civilization to fruition, there will be a struggle with the status quo. This is to say many people will not like the changing energy or the changing thoughts. There will be struggle and strife resulting in violence. What is referred to in Revelations as the End of Days will be the death of the old patterns of beliefs as we shake off the chaos created by old thoughts and a slower, lower vibration. There is pain with birth and growth. We cannot look at the death of the old as something to be mourned when we can celebrate the birth of the new age. Those people who can handle the vibration will stay. Those who cannot will not be coming back to the earth plane but rather going to another "Earth" to continue to work from that plane of existence.

It is our responsibility to help others let go of old doctrine, dogmatic paradigms, and racially charged ideology. Working toward bringing balance into mind, body, and spirit will create more light for those who follow. Fear, violence, anger, and bigotry cannot live in the same space as enlightenment.

INTEGRATION

We grow in spiritual knowledge as the collective consciousness evolves. Buddha lived six centuries before Jesus and also attained the Christ consciousness. One of the precepts for the Aquarian Age is that Jesus will step down as the "reigning Christ" as soon as humans see each other as equals. At that point, Buddha will become the "reigning Christ consciousness." Jesus' reign as the Christ consciousness came first as he was the healing Christ. He taught us that we have to heal in mind, body, and spirit. Buddha attained the Christ consciousness and his gift to us was his ability to understand humankind. This gift is to see each other as equals. How can we see each other as equals if we have not done the work of healing first?

This is not to say that we can't all evolve past the teachings of Buddha; however, that would require many Buddhists, Christians, Muslims, Hindus, etc., to give up their current religious teachings and beliefs to open to a higher level of consciousness than is offered through religious/spiritual dogma.

At this time, we are in the middle of higher consciousness emerging. Many people call it the "Great Awakening" while still others call it the "Great Divide." We are in strife politically all across the world. In America, people are torn between two parties with neither giving an inch socially (the death of George Floyd, the recognition of the suppression of people of color, women's body autonomy) and physically (people fighting about wearing masks with the pandemic raging around us). It is much the same across the world with people fighting wars on many fronts also.

It is our time for awakening to the higher truths of who we are and what we have created for ourselves through conscious creation. As noted in this chapter, if you truly believe in reincarnation, you have been black, brown, red, yellow, and white. You have been rich and poor. You have enslaved and been enslaved. You have been heterosexual, homosexual, bisexual, transgender, and everything in between, including asexual. You have died old and died young. You have raped, murdered, and pillaged. You have been raped, murdered, and pillaged. There isn't one thing you haven't been or experienced. What you did with and through it, how you reacted to it, and what you have yet to learn from it will be seen through the next few years.

I encourage you to open your hearts and your minds and quit fighting through this time. It is a time for self-healing so your light will be felt helping others who are unable to let go of their fears, anger, pain, and grief. Remember, from the aspect of judgment, we are to use it as a tool to help ourselves grow spiritually, not as a sword to stab each other.

Chapter Seven

UNIVERSAL LOVE

There is a difference between the love the God-Source has for us and the way we love as humans. The love the God-Source holds for us is universal. It is unconditional love, strong, pure, and contains no human emotions. This is why the God-Source allows "bad things to happen to good people" (remember, it isn't the God-Source that creates those experiences). It is only through experiencing all that is good and all that is bad that humanity can differentiate between the two. With the experiences of good and bad, we learn our lessons and progress until, eventually, we return to the Sea of Bliss with the God-Source.

Humans have created different aspects of love. Each aspect gives more insight and truth toward reaching the understanding and acceptance of universal love for ourselves and others. To have universal love, we must first let go of judgment, guilt, fear, and anger for ourselves and others.

Our heart chakra is a key aspect to higher consciousness. Many of us have experienced the opening of the heart chakra, but to hold it open for long stretches, or forever, is a goal we should be working toward. The heart chakra (emotion) is the middle ground between the lower self (physical body), survival needs, with the higher self and its spiritual (philosophical) needs. The heart chakra is where our emotions, which create our feelings, are found and expressed. It is the link to the emotional body and, when it is opened, the spiritual and physical bodies come into balance.

Universal love is the unconditional love of everything and everyone. There are no exceptions, there are no judgments, there is only acceptance. There is no anger, only understanding. There is no fear, only compassion. In other words, **there is no emotion**, there is only the moment of now and being in unconditional love.

Universal love holds no separation. It doesn't express itself through loving one person, place, or thing more than another. With universal (unconditional) love, all things are loved and experienced equally through that love. To help us find universal love, we have had many different experiences of love in order to bring the truth of love to light. Each aspect of love teaches us more and more about love. Understanding each aspect is only an avenue, not separate from any other love, which teaches us the divinity of love.

Let us look at some of the aspects of love. Our first love experience is love of parents. We are born and, hopefully, we bond with our parents. Even if we are adopted there can be bonding. This bonding is created when the heart chakra of the parents tied to the heart chakra of the incarnating child. This is a reciprocal sharing of heart energy. It is rare for a child to deny their parents. A parent holds power over the child due to the responsibility of caring for the child.

Love of a child

From the moment a child and parent meet, the bond is created (there are times the bonding is incomplete). This presents problems for the child as he/she ages. The creation of this bond starts within the opening of the heart chakra as they meet. The parent(s) feel a protective love and a responsibility to take care of the basic needs of the child: providing food, shelter, and clothing. Language is taught and behavioral standards are expected. This is how the child learns about the expectations of the earth plane. Yes, sometimes there are harsh lessons, sometimes there are not, but they are karmic lessons nonetheless.

We have all heard how codependency is unhealthy. The parent/

child love is possibly one of the best examples of codependent love we have. Because it is the parents' responsibility to teach the child about societal standards, the parents will often feel guilty when the child fails to meet the expectations, and the parent will brag when the child excels. Codependent love feeds off of itself. The perceived weaknesses or failures in their children's ability to accept their responsibilities for their lives on the earth plane grate on the parents' hearts. For children to operate effectively in their destinies, they must learn to accept hard knocks and to learn what works and what doesn't. For example, if a child steals a candy bar and the parent pays for it because of embarrassment, the child learns he/she can continue stealing, and the parent will continue to be embarrassed and continue to bail the child out of trouble. This is often done because the parent doesn't want to be seen as lacking in parental skills. However, we have all heard the saying, "Spare the rod, spoil the child." I don't agree with striking anyone, but I do think we can change this verbiage to say, "Spare the accountability and the child will rot."

Love of pets

Loving your pet is simple. The pet loves you unconditionally and without judgment. They are like a very young child, without guile and with an open heart. Our reciprocal love is faithful companionship and care, or at least it should be. We have all heard people say, "It's just a dog… cat… hamster, etc." When I hear those words, I have to recognize this person does not understand that our pets are spiritual beings also. We fell to our level of "Rebellion," and they fell to theirs. They have their realm they have to work upward through and we have ours. To deny they have spirits and souls is to forget the truth of what and who we are as well.

Love of a partner/mate

As we grow and mature on the physical plane, we take on a partner. Sometimes this is a life partner, sometimes they're only in our lives for a period of time. The only rules that apply on the earth plane are karma and destiny. We learn through our partner relationships how to coexist. There are always things to be learned when we share space. It helps us learn to strengthen our weaknesses and soften our strengths. We learn more about ourselves when we have someone showing us a mirror reflecting us back to ourselves. Remember the Johari's Window? Above all the other types of love, partnerships can help us shrink the second window, our blind spot.

Sexual Love

The mating ritual helps us to release negative energy that has built up in our systems. It helps, through orgasm especially, to balance the physical body hormones. Balancing our hormones helps us to be healthy. Feeling good in the physical sense helps to balance the mind and spirit. The same thing applies when the spirit is balanced. When we talk about chakras, we will understand how important balance is. Suffice it to say, the release of negative energy from the body brings about a more balanced, stable life.

There are many other types of love: love of country, love of activity, love of objects, and love of ideals. All of these loves hold a key to the understanding of perfect love, universal love. When we release expectations and judgments, our mortal love transmutes and becomes unconditional/universal love.

Love and Its Triggers

Marriage - (plus 1)
Birth - (plus 1 or more)
New Job - (more income)
New Home - (financial increase and stability)
New Country - (more possibilities)
Good Health - (feel good)
Love of Creatures - (awareness of other sentient life forms)

When we look at the list of love and possible triggers, we see an addition to our life. In our simplistic way of viewing life, negative equates to loss or change. Whereas with love we see it as a multiplication of happiness. Yet it all is still created by change. Our fear of loss in the future often cuts off our enjoyment of the present.

Opening our hearts to love is the highest, most positive vibration to be in when we are creating opportunities for healing. Fear comes before all negative emotions. With that in mind, to let go of our fear and feel love, we need to understand and become accountable for that which we fear.

Fears and Possible Triggers

Fear of losing a loved one - (death, divorce)

Fear of losing financial stability - (job or income)

Fear of losing home - (catastrophe, financial)

Fear of losing country - (war, moving)

Fear of losing health - (injury, illness, death)

Fear of losing happiness - (loss of any kind, mental illness)

Fear of creatures - (spiders, snakes)

Fear of heights - (falling)

If you look at the list, most of it has to do with immediate loss and all of it has to do with changes in circumstances. A spider may bite you. You will get ill and die. Loss of life steps in. So we view fears as a "taking away" from our status quo.

Fear is often described by the acronym; **F**alse **E**vidence **A**ppearing **R**eal. The media explodes with stories designed to captivate our attention. What better way to sell a story than to sell fear? We thrive on these stories because we want/need to understand how another conquered the fear scenario. We elect the best politician who proves to us they will keep us from harm's way. We keep creating instances where fear takes hold. However, we need to face our fears, let go of negativity and embrace the positive.

What we fear most we create to overcome that fear. Fear is negative and holds no value. Sometimes it keeps us alive, but only because we fear dying. We are taught to fear pain and death. If we actually realized death is but an actual birth back to our true expression, then we would no longer fear it. It is the irrational fears that we hold onto that are left to control and negate that block our advancement. For instance, when we marry, do we think of getting a divorce or that we may lose a partner? No, of course not. We are looking to a bright future. If we thought we were going to lose the person we married, would we forego the experience of loving them? Why live in a state of fear which brings us so much in the way of negativity when we can embrace all that is good and live in peace and harmony, bringing forth all that is positive?

Another way fear takes hold is through media exploitation. We listen to stories of bombings or stories of a drug cartel in another country. We do not want to accept refugees in this country because we fear they might bring those circumstances they are fleeing to our doorsteps. If you truly understand you are going to die at one point anyway, why do you fear the loss of your life to such a degree that you fear how it might happen? That takes us out of our heart chakras being open with universal love. It negates it so much that the chakra door slams shut. Fear is a pointless waste of energy. Fear of dying before our time or in a manner **not** predestined may be understandable, but also senseless.

Universal love connects us to the universal mind, our God-Source. That connection brings with it our gifts of spirit to bring about world change. Loving purely and divinely is the greatest gift of all. It moves us from the idea of what is for the good of self and into the realization of the good of all.

INTEGRATION

I first wrote these chapters to teach classes. At the time of the writing, I had two living children. It was easy for me to get into the flow of understanding universal love because I hadn't experienced a severe shock to my spiritual system. I have had my heart chakra open at different times in my life. I have also had it slammed shut. It wasn't until the death of my son that I had to work tirelessly to reconnect spiritually with others again. I have experienced other losses on many levels throughout my life. I have contemplated the why of these many times. What I have realized is that to know and understand your fellow human beings, you must understand what it is they have undergone in their lives that has shaped them into who they are today. It is taught that Buddha knows humanity far better than any other Christed one. His enlightenment came through the study of humanity.

What better way to learn of pure, divine love than to begin to understand humanity? How can we fully appreciate the beauty of someone when we don't completely accept them, foibles and all? To fully bring healing or to have compassion, we need to walk in their shoes so we don't judge them. Having gone through loss, we recognize the defensive measure we hold around our hearts. Loss triggers fear. Fear shuts down our heart chakras. If we are to bring healing to ourselves, we must also see where we are accountable for the creation of our own pain. It isn't necessary to have an understanding of someone's pain, because it is there for them to learn from. We don't need to take on their karmic choices. Understanding someone's pain allows compassion. It's compassion, not empathy or sympathy, that allows the person to shift into the healing space.

Empathy and Sympathy

While these two concepts are not discussed in the first portion of this chapter on universal love, it is important we discuss them in the integration. Empathy and sympathy are aspects of mortal love. Universal love is pure and divine. It holds compassion, not sympathy or empathy.

Many people call themselves empaths. They may or may not be. I am going to offer you a different view of concepts: Empaths feel the pain, dizziness, and illness of others as if he/she is experiencing it. For example, someone walks into the room with a headache. The empath will suddenly feel the onslaught of a headache. However, being empathetic is different. We can put ourselves in another's shoes and understand what that person is going through, but we do not actually feel their physical, mental, or emotional sensations. There is a HUGE difference.

Sympathy is pretty much a useless tool for healing. I will give you the explanation of the word "sympathy" as I read it in a book at a young age. I quote, "In the dictionary, sympathy is found between shit and syphilis," in other words, it is a useless emotion. This was such a reality check for me. It has kept me clear of many co-dependent situations that I might have gotten embroiled in. Leave sympathy to the Hallmark cards and embrace unconditional love and compassion for every person, animal, place, and thing.

CHAPTER EIGHT

PRECEPTS

Precepts are general rules intended to raise the consciousness of humankind by setting goals to be attained by humanity. At the beginning of every age (2,100 years) Sages, both discarnate (those in spirit) and incarnate (those currently living a life on Earth), who are wise and judicious, gather together to set the precepts for the forthcoming age. In this Aquarian Age, 13 Sages met in 1977. The names of the Sages (both of spirit and human) are unknown. This is probably to protect those who happen to be incarnated on Earth at the time they met. It could also be the identities are not revealed because we tend to either deify those who are thought to be ascended masters or crucify them.

As we become more fully ensconced in the Aquarian Age, the precepts for this age will be made known. You will see the shift in consciousness in humankind as we work toward those precepts. The precepts are formulated according to how far mankind has progressed in the preceding age. These precepts give us guidelines for our destiny paths. Think of the precepts as a goal to meet in order to bring forth higher truths. When these precepts are formulated, our spirit teachers/ guides work diligently to help their mortal charges work toward them.

The Sages do not give the precepts to the masses. It is our Free Will combined with our destiny plan that help us to attain higher knowledge and to grow spiritually to meet those precepts. Precepts set the tone for the age. Past ages are reviewed, and the energy and spiritual awakening of the collective consciousness is taken. The precepts can be looked at as either benchmarks to mark our progression collectively or as goals to be attained individually. There would be no point in setting precepts if they aren't attainable by the masses.

The Aquarian Age dawned in 1962. The energies of both the Piscean Age and the Aquarian Age were felt and in effect from that time until more recently - approximately 2014. The energies feel much like the shadow phase of a retrograde. A shadow phase is a time just before the beginning and a bit of time after the end of the event itself. In the beginning, the shadow phase helps to build the energy to help bring the event (the age) in, and, at the end, it helps to slowly drop the energy of the event (age) leaving. At the end of the Piscean Age, the energy was declining at the same time the energy of the Aquarian Age was building.

As stated previously, the precepts for this age were set in 1977. After much thought and meditation, it has been revealed that one of the precepts will be for each person to have universal/unconditional love for ourselves and others. You can see this starting to happen now. Our actions and struggles currently are toward racial and gender equality. As we become more globally interactive, we begin to see connections to other cultures and communities as learning and growing opportunities instead of a fear of loss or control. However, as much as we would like to think it, we are not nearly as far along as we should be. We create our current communities with leadership that stimulates our fears. This is why it is easy to see universal love as a precept for the Aquarian Age. Universal love will be necessary for everyone to go back to the Sea of Bliss.

In every age prior to the Aquarian Age, there has been a Christ. A Christ is a being who has reached a level of awareness of truth that we refer to as the "Christ consciousness." In the past, this spiritual being agreed to incarnate to give teachings to help the other incarnating entities reach the precepts as set forth by the sages. Many Christs have returned to the earth plane to help us but have ended up failing their destiny and falling back down the rabbit hole. As far as is known, there have been 144 entities who have attained the Christ consciousness. They incarnated to help us find truth, and some of them regressed. Therefore, in the Aquarian Age there will be no Christ to lead us. There may be enlightened ones to help us along, but, for the most part, we are on our own to help ourselves and others as best we can.

Another possible precept will be faith. We often misconstrue faith as a dedicated belief we hold toward the God-Source. The extension of the concept of faith is the knowing of truths. With that will come a greater understanding of our God gifts and our abilities to use them correctly. We will see with clairvoyance (our third eye), hear with clairaudience (our spiritual ear), and will know the spirit of the God-Source. If we are better able to use our God gifts, we will be closer to the light and will be able to hear the wisdom and guidance from our spirit teachers/guides without relying on someone else's interpretation or accuracy. This will increase our ability to be accountable for our actions and bring us into more balance with our karmic debts.

Unfortunately, mortals have a tendency to deify the Christed One and fail to embrace and work toward attaining and applying the teachings for themselves. The eighth ray was cast to help raise our consciousness. Think of the rays as a vibration, or frequency or if it is easier, think of the musical notes on the scales. The scales start at one note and climb up. This is how the rays work. The more rays, the higher the vibration, and the more the light of truth is realized. As the eighth ray was implemented in our world, it increased the global vibration or frequency. As the vibration/frequency increases, it raises our vibrations and brings more light of truth to us. Those who cannot handle this higher vibration will cease incarnating on the earth plane. Another planet has been prepared for those people who leave. They will not just vanish from here and go there; they will pass back into the etheric until the time comes for their next incarnation. It will be at that time they go to the other planet.

This does not mean that everyone who dies, no matter the circumstances of their death, cannot handle the higher vibration. There will be those who are passing back into the etheric because it is their time and destiny to do so. There will be others whose deaths are an accident.

INTEGRATION

When I first studied Precepts, I wanted to know who the Sages were, where they met, what Precepts they made and why. If we are to create universal love for ourselves and others, it follows that one of the Precepts is trust. Exchange the word "trust" with "faith" if it feels better to you. "Faith" is a word associated with religion and lends itself to the concept that faith is complete trust in someone or something, it also holds the energy of belief. The word "trust" in metaphysics is a knowing, not a belief or an action.

The evidence showing up through society now is one where universal love is being called in; therefore, through the classes offered at the spiritualist church I trained at, one of the Precepts is about universal or unconditional love. We will touch upon the concept because it has to do with the "governing Christ consciousness." Jesus came to guide us through the Piscean Age. He came here to show us how important it was to heal ourselves and others. He is known as the "Healing Christ." He also taught us about loving one another, healing, and about the various gifts of spirit we have the capabilities to do.

Acts 2:17 - "In the last days, God says, I will pour out my Spirit on all people. Your sons and daughters will prophesy, your young men will see visions, your old men will dream dreams. "

I am not saying the end of days is near. We won't quit working with this planet until we have attained the Christ consciousness. Acts 2:17 is talking about the last days of the Piscean Age which ended in 1962. Have you noticed more people are embracing their gifts of spirit? They are also more accepting of others' gifts. It is a step up vibrationally. However, there won't be a human Christed one in the Aquarian Age. Jesus and his teachings are the reigning Christ consciousness right now. It won't be until humankind sees one another as equals and as brothers/ sisters that Buddha will become the reigning Christ consciousness. The Christ consciousness is a reference to the level of awareness attained through spiritual progression.

Buddha in the form of the Christ consciousness does not mean that we will all become Buddhists. It does mean that his teachings will be the governing consciousness when he ascends to the position of reigning Christ consciousness, just as Jesus' teachings are the governing consciousness now. Not everyone is a Christian, but every religion has similar teachings. In the Aquarian Age, we will be doing away with formal religious teachings and dogma. We will be embracing spiritual paths. Churches will become meditation facilities if they exist at all.

To reiterate regarding the eighth ray. Think of it as a raising of the vibration of human consciousness. Currently, humankind is at level seven. As the vibration continues to rise, we will move to level eight and then to level nine. I was taught in 1992, that in 1993 the eighth ray would be cast. The term "cast" means raising the vibration and frequency which would foster raising human consciousness. It is by evidence of the shifts that happened for people, that I believe the eighth ray was cast somewhere between 1992 and 1996. I encourage you to look back during that four-year window. You may note something of major importance happened to you and you shifted your perspective mentally, emotionally, and spiritually. In my case, I started studying at Universal Church of the Holy Spirit, a spiritualist church here in Albuquerque. The ninth ray was to be cast sometime between 2012 and 2015. You may have noticed another shift in your life. Astrologically a lot was happening, and during that time something of major importance may have happened to you. In 2015 I was told I was coming back to the United States, where I would open my metaphysics center and start teaching.

CHAPTER NINE

HUMAN ASPECTS

As we know, everything is vibration. Vibrations are mathematical. Everywhere on this planet we see the number 7. There are seven days of the week, seven chakras or psychic centers, seven colors of the spectrum, and seven notes to complete a scale. The number 7 is found in the Bible 735 times, 54 times in Revelations alone. 7 is the number of completeness and perfection, both physically and spiritually. In the future, the number for humans will increase to 8 then 9, and continue to rise to 12 as the rays of energy increase.

Aspects of One – Union

One of the oldest symbols of God-Source from humankind is a point within a circle. The circle represents the circumference of being. Included in the beingness are wisdom, life, and love without a beginning or end. The point within the circle represents the higher self, the divine mind. Mortals are the microcosm or manifestation of the higher self. To know, to understand the higher self is the work of eternities. This point within the circle is the symbol for man in the God-Source's image, that of spirit.

If you think about this, you will realize the point within the circle is found even in the smallest form of life, the cell. Our physical form is composed of trillions of tiny cells which regenerate constantly. It takes seven years for every cell in every organ of the body to regenerate completely. This is further evidence of humankind resonating as a 7. Wherever you look throughout the universe you will see the circle with a point inside resembling that of a cell.

The Universe is one grand harmonious union, one mind, one substance, one principle, one universal spirit tied to one life, one truth, and one True Source. We are a part of the God-Source; therefore, we are the God-Source. We are one and the same with the God-Source. It is the Universal Law of Divine Oneness. As the law says, we are one with all plants, animals, human beings, and cosmic beings. With this oneness we co-create.

Aspects of Two – Duality

Within humanity is a duality. There is much to be gleaned from our duality. While we hold within our beings the image of the light of the Creator, we are also mortal and have a physical form. Within the construct of our physical bodies, we express that duality. There are both male (positive polarity) and female (negative polarity) aspects to our physical duality. The right brain expresses the emotion, creativity and the feminine energies, while the left brain expresses the masculine, or logic. Our two nervous systems, the central and autonomic, are expressed in the same manner. The central is masculine and the autonomic is the feminine where emotions are manifested. The heart has four chambers, or, if you will, two halves, an intake and an output, which are also halved.

In Chapter 2, when our creation was discussed, we were both male and female. We started possessing all the animals' bodies, which is to say we pushed out their spirits and then our spirits entered their bodies to experience the earth plane through them. It wasn't until we incarnated, which entailed possessing the anthropoid apes in utero in order to go through the birthing process, that caused the split into positive and negative polarity began. This split of our original selves gave us our "soulmates," or our other halves. The masculine expression is the "director/manager" of the experience, while the feminine expression is designed to deal with the emotional experience. Our true other halves, or our soulmates, stay in spirit while we incarnate and vice versa.

We live in an amoral universe. We are good and evil, light and dark, higher and lower consciousness. This is part of our duality. Instead of understanding the duality, we have placed limitations on our expression of it. Limiting our expression of duality is a form of self-negation. It is through this limitation that we make mistakes and break the universal laws. As we unfold in spiritual knowledge, we progress. The more we progress, the more the beauty of our structure will unfold. Truth and love will start to manifest. The negativity in our lives will fall away, and the unity of the physical with the spiritual bodies will happen.

To know our true selves, we need to recognize our duality. The lower self is expressed through the vibrations of the first, second, and third chakras. The higher self expresses through the vibrations of the fifth, sixth, and seventh chakras. The link between the lower and higher selves is the vibration of the fourth chakra. The fourth chakra is the heart chakra which governs universal love. The lower self has its uses for now, but, eventually, as our consciousness rises, we will no longer need to learn the lessons of those chakras through negative expressions or experiences.

Aspects of Three – Mind, Body, Spirit

The threefold aspect of mortals is comprised of spirit, soul, and body. The number 3 is used to represent the higher self while the number 4 is used to represent the foundation of the lower self. The Tabernacle, which is a sanctuary in Jerusalem, was formed on the number 3. The Holy of Holies (our inner spiritual nature where our light rests), the Holy Place, (which holds our higher self), and the Holy Court (Akasha where our report card, our soul progression, lies).

Aspects of Four – Foundations

As stated above, the 4 symbolizes the foundation upon which the higher self rests. The fourth chakra is expressed as universal love and the link between the lower and higher selves. Eventually this number will be transformed, so we cannot look at it as the "middle ground number" but as a necessary component through which we measure our progress at this time. It is a limited state of consciousness or being. It is the representation of the physical form, of the density necessary for us to comprehend the material plane.

Aspects of Five – Humanity

Found in the 5 are the aspects of humanity and are represented as the five-pointed star. Some say 5 represents man in direct contrast to matter. 5 is dual in that it brings both complements of joy and sorrow. This occurs according to how we use the energy of 5. Understanding the contrast may help you to comprehend more clearly the karmic aspects. We learn by doing, and we have both good and bad to show the contrast. We need to understand how we experience our karmic debts which will also determine how quickly we pay those debts. The number 5 stands as nature's number and is symbolized by the pentagram, which shows the figure of a man, the head in the spiritual, or north, node, arms outstretched, one to the east and the other to the west, with the feet planted firmly on the Earth. When we finally know ourselves, we will be able to distinguish between the lower and the higher selves, and our pentagram will shine brightly with the joy of truth.

Aspects of Six – Human Divinity

The symbolic representation for 6 is the double triangle. One triangle has its apex pointing up. This is symbolic of the God-Source and the highest spiritual aspects. The other triangle has its apex pointing down. This represents the creation of the universe and Man. The number 6 is also the number for error and temptation, toil, and punishment. You can see other dualities: spirit + temptation = humans; toil + punishment = karmic debt. All of these traits of mankind can be overcome. This is an example of where ego, when used correctly, can triumph with the use of good judgment from the higher self and bring us back into balance.

Aspects of Seven – Attaining God Consciousness

Understand that we start recognizing our divineness with the seventh aspect of humanity. It brings us to the realization that we are a part of the God-Source, therefore we are the God-Source, or we are Divine. The symbol for the number 7 is the combination of the square (four-sided foundational base) and triangle (three-sided figure) with the apex pointing upward to what most people understand is heaven. This is the number that man vibrates to at this time. It is the key to the whole life of the ego.

We can take comfort in the thought the lower self, symbolized by the number 4 (the 4-sided base) will eventually blend, transforming into the 7 with the help of the triangle (3-sided figure), manifesting into the higher self. When humanity allows the God-self to guide life, life becomes less dramatic and more complete. It is then that our pain and suffering will end. We can choose to pay our karmic debt straight down our destiny path with joy or can make it a winding path of pain and suffering. To get off the karmic wheel, evolution of the spirit is necessary, and we have free will to choose which way we will experience our path.

INTEGRATION

We need to understand the human aspects of humankind. When we don't understand ourselves, we create conflict within ourselves and between each other. Fear, greed, and power become all that is desirable for us to attain. This is so we do not become oppressed. If we understand the aspects, then we can let go of the unknown factors that bring fear. We can embrace the higher knowledge, allowing it to integrate so we may step up even further in consciousness. We shouldn't have to have protests demanding rights that are already ours by being human. We also shouldn't have to quantify the oppression of others. We need to recognize we have been where they are now and hold a space of compassion for them.

I want to emphasize the higher and lower selves. To clarify, when we first incarnated, humans had to find food, shelter, and the basics of life to survive. This is associated with the energy of the first chakra. The second chakra is the basic life force evolving into humanity. It is identified with our sexual expression. As a group consciousness, we are in the energy of the third chakra. When the third chakra is flowing in the positive direction, a person is a master of their emotions, calm, and brave. In relationships, the third chakra should remain flowing in the positive direction, allowing both partners to feel they are masters of their emotions and capable of being equal partners. When flowing in the negative direction, a person can't share. Creativity is stifled. Emotions are shut down. A person is cowardly (as in yellow belly). Fear governs actions and sex feels threatening. There is difficulty giving and receiving. Digesting food can be problematic and possibly cause weight problems.

This is where the world is today. With all of the anger, fear, and pain, people are pushing every button they can to stimulate that fear so that our fears are put on display for us to look at. It is only through our self-observation and accountability that we can bring about much needed healing for ourselves.

There are so many people fixated on the fourth, fifth, and sixth dimensions. Don't be one of them. Understand that you are incarnated at this time for a reason. That reason is to bring light to this third dimension. I am going to repeat it, WE CHOSE to come here at this time.

Achieving total perfection on the earth plane is impossible. We will progress to another plane of existence. Think of Earth as the elementary school. You cannot graduate high school from elementary school.

SELF ACTIVATION

CHAPTER TEN

ANGELS, SPIRIT TEACHERS, GUIDES, AND GUARDIANS

Jesus

Humans at one time or another, in one life or another, could see auras. As humans, we work toward spiritual unfoldment. Our chakras flow positive and negative depending on our thoughts and emotions. When flowing positive, the colors of the chakras are vibrant and beautiful. When flowing negative, the color can be dark, murky, and streaked. When a chakra is sluggish, the color may be partially vibrant while still having some streaks or murkiness. The combined colors of all seven of the chakras when fully opened is a beautiful white light. The head chakras (1,000 lights) shine brightly, making a "halo." It was because Jesus had reached the Christ consciousness and had all his chakras open that Jesus' captors placed a crown of thorns upon his head. This was to close his connection to his higher self.

When Jesus incarnated, his destiny was to bring forth the knowledge of healing. As a clairvoyant, he could see with his third eye open that people had balanced their karma through illness and injury. He was then able to provide healing for their condition. Hence, he was called the "Healing Christ."

With spiritual progression, we too will have the ability to help ourselves and others. This knowledge of the truth of who we are also allows us to know the truth of our own immortality and eternal beings of light. The more we let go of fear, the more we will become accountable for our own paths.

We are now at a time when there will be no mortal Christs to follow with their teachings. Once we see all as equal and look to each other as brothers/sisters, Buddha will take Jesus' place as the Christ consciousness and his teachings will help us to further progress. The vibration will be high enough so we will be able to attain enlightenment through our own accountability and progression.

Angels

The term "angel" should not be used synonymously with "guide," "guardian," and "teacher." They are not the same. These beings are as different from one another as their functions/jobs are.

Angles do not leave the Sea of Bliss. Think of them as the white around the yolk of an egg. The yolk is the point of creation. The white supports and protects the yolk (source of creation).

We are often taught to believe that angels are entities with wings and halos who do God's bidding and who drop in to give us aid and succor. It is not angels who interact with us on Earth but rather our spirit guides/teachers/guardians and loved ones who have crossed over.

Elohim

The Elohim are seven orders of angels who stand closest to the center of creation. They are the angels in charge of our chakras. In each order, one has been assigned a center. As we raise our consciousness and our vibration rises in frequency, our chakras start to connect to the Elohim order in charge of that particular chakra. For example, when we first incarnated, we needed to obtain food and shelter and learn to survive. That is the energy of the first chakra. The Elohim order that is in charge of that chakra brings the lesson of the chakra to all of us for us to learn to hold that chakra in positive expression for ourselves. The chakras will be further explained in the chapter on chakras.

The Archangels

There isn't just one Archangel Michael or Gabriel. They are an order or group of archangels. They have their own status and responsibilities. They are in the Sea of Bliss and work within that frame of the realm.

- **The Michaels** - mete out justice on a group level. There are many groups in this world. We have religious groups, cultural groups, professions, and people grouped in categories of age, likes, and dislikes. These are just some examples. Sometimes we get into what we call the "mob mentality," meaning that a group will hold fear in their hearts. One of the jobs of the Michaels is to help people break free of fear by helping the group through karmic balancing.

- **The Gabriels** - call us at death's door. Throughout life, there are many death experiences. Even if we are leaving one job for another that was tailor-made for us, there is a death experience. We leave people we have learned to know and work with. There is also a death when a child moves out of the house for whatever reason. The Gabriels help us move the energy from one of ending with grief to one of beginning with joy and celebration. At the time of physical death, they call on us to help us finalize our life experiences.

- **The Raphaels** - hold the keys to the universal mind (knowledge). It is the Raphaels who, when we have attained the right level of spiritual enlightenment, bring the knowledge of the Universe, the truth of who we are and where we came from to us. The Universal Mind is unlocked by the "keys of knowledge." We must always seek the highest level of truth we can understand, then we, too, will be rewarded with the keys.

- **The Uriels** – The name Uriel means "God is my light." We don't know much about the Uriels. However, through trance teachings, they are involved with the occult entities (Occult entities are of the highest order). They are associated with repenting. Therefore, it stands to reason they help humanity through group karma, which is a large-scale karmic balancing of nations, societies, and planets.

- **Grim Reapers** - meet us when our physical bodies die. They escort us back to the etheric, or what is commonly known as Heaven. There is not just one grim reaper. They are an order, just as all angels are. When we die, we are still attached to the physical body by a silver cord. It takes three days for the cord to dissolve and for our spirit to be released. This is why we used to sit with the body, and funerals are still held three days after death. The Grim Reaper comes to escort you back to the etheric once the cord dissipates.

  As we pass, often loved ones from our current lives come to meet us at our death. They embrace us. This helps to alleviate the fear of the transition. Sometimes death is so unexpected and the cord is dissolved too quickly, by fire for example, that we are released from the physical form and become lost. It is these deceased ones that might become ghosts. Remember there is the astral body that can look like a haunting until it fades. The astral body is seen as doing normal, everyday functions repeatedly, such as making breakfast or sitting in a chair reading.

- **Seraphim** - We are from this order. We "fell," or left the Sea of Bliss, through what is called the Rebellion. Only a part of the Seraphim Order left. Lucifer, who was an Elohim, talked the Seraphim and other orders of angels into leaving the Sea of Bliss and believing we were equal in power to the God-Source. Because we are from the Sea of Bliss, we are a part of the God-Source and, therefore, co-creators with the God-Source. This means that we are co-creating our life experiences with each other on Earth in the NOW.

- **Cherubim** - We are unsure of their duties at this time. None from their order left the Sea of Bliss, meaning they did not fall on any level. They might be the protectors of the edges of the Sea of Bliss, similar to the membrane of the cell. Just as the membrane softens to allow nutrients to come in and nourish the cell, as a metaphor, the nutrient of love may cross through the border to sustain the connection between our true selves and the God-Source. The Cherubim have something to do with helping us attain universal love.

Guide aka Guardian Angel

Everyone has a guardian angel. This is our guide. We only have one. Our guide commits to helping us from birth to death. When we have the desire to unfold, we attract our other teachers to help us in our progression. Our guide will impress upon us, for example, to exit the freeway. Then later we find out that had we continued on the freeway we might have been in a horrible accident. They help us miss the potholes which would not serve our higher selves or our destinies. If we ignore them, we may find ourselves in disastrous situations which are completely unnecessary to our current experience. They are the ones who, as we need further guidance, will help call upon those teachers who can best help us, our guides and our teachers have had past lives with us and have progressed to a level of understanding that they use to help us progress.

Spirit Teachers

Spirit teachers are individual spirit beings who, like us, have had incarnations on Earth. When they pass back into the etheric from having lived on Earth, they made the decision to train to qualify so they may assist us while we are in human form. They devote their time, energy, intellect, and their own experiences to help humankind progress. They, too, are working to go back to the Sea of Bliss. It is in the manner of being a teacher that they work to progress on their paths to get back to the Sea of Bliss. A spirit teacher is not above your guide or vice versa. It is just the roles they have chosen to play to help us. They have a connection to us, usually through having experienced a life, or possibly many lives, with us. It is our level of understanding that determines the status/knowledge of our spirit teachers and guide. As we grow and unfold, our teachers guide us. Once we reach a level of awareness at which they can no longer help us, other teachers will come in to take their places by our side. The old teacher will step out until he/she is needed or will move on. When you do not have the need for the expertise of one teacher, that teacher has work they can do in spirit as well as help other humans. They do not remain idle just waiting for you. This is why it is important to only call upon them when their particular brand of expertise is needed.

Our teachers are divided into seven major categories, one for each psychic center, also known as chakras. There are general names for each category of teacher to better understand their function. Do not misunderstand, the names and categories are only to help us understand the area of work in which they work and in no way speak to the level of advancement they have attained. A messenger could very easily be an advanced being. This is true even on Earth. Just because someone is homeless, it does not speak to the level of spiritual knowledge they carry, nor does the smartest person necessarily have the highest level of spiritual knowledge.

Our guides and teachers do not hinder or stop us from our responsibilities. They do not restrict the use of our free will. They instruct, guide, and lead us in any and every way they can to help us fulfill our karmic obligations, follow our destiny, and progress spiritually. Our major responsibility is to meet the level of understanding we had attained in our prior lives and to progress further. To do this we (with the help of our guide and teachers) create a destiny before we decide to incarnate. Help comes from our guides and teachers to keep us on our paths, even though we make mistakes. When we think we are alone, we are not. Everything we say, do, and think is heard or felt by at least one of our spirit helpers. To reiterate, our spirit teachers are attracted to us in accordance with our needs, merits, and progression.

The earth plane is of lower vibration and dense. We struggle with staying on our path. Think of the Earth as a grade school. In first grade we stumble through trying to learn procedures and protocol. In second grade we know where the bathrooms are, our reading has improved, but our comprehension is still low. Third grade brings a better vocabulary and our responsibilities increase. This growth and understanding continue until we have reached a state of consciousness where we can graduate. To graduate from this plane of existence, we must attain the Christ consciousness. The Christ consciousness is a level of spiritual progression in which we can work with all our spirit gifts and hold unconditional love for all beings without ego. We would be able to transmute our bodies from the physical form into the ethers. An entire book could be written on the Christ consciousness.

Our spiritual helpers can be viewed as the community of elders. When we get ourselves into situations that may take us off of our paths, they will impress upon us the right choices to make. This is one reason it is wise to develop intuition. Without this guidance, we would not be able to make it through life. They embrace us with warm reassurance when we are distressed. They use inspiration to keep us motivated and strong. They have all had lives on the Earth, so they understand our human nature and our situations. They have progressed and are willing to help at every turn. However, we do have to remember to ask for help and say thank you when we receive it. Keep in mind it is OUR "free will" decisions. It is at this time when our teachers stand back. It is up to us to make a decision in the very best way that we can. We may feel very alone at these times, but we are not.

Spiritual Teachers and Your Material Needs

One of the driving needs on Earth is money. This and love are the two mandates WE feel are necessary to make our lives better. When we seek monetary abundance, we forget that we may have some karma with money. For example, we may not have been good stewards of money in other lives. We may have been greedy, a spendthrift, or money could have possibly created such a nice life that we became lazy, causing us to forget why we were truly here. It could also be we don't deem ourselves worthy of abundance in this life, so we create a life of lack.

Another form of currency in other lives was bartering. It was the tool for the exchange of services. This shows that money was not necessary to feed ourselves or our families. In spirit, we understand there is no lack, only abundance. While on Earth, we create our world from our thoughts and what we have learned from our families. If, for example, you think you need to experience lack, you will. We are the creators of every moment of our lives. Not having enough can make someone angry and they will regress. At the same time, having abundance may also make us angry and regress. Each of us experiences what we decide to create so we progress spiritually. This does not mean you should not work toward creating a large abundance. What it does mean is what you think, you will create.

Asking for your spirit teachers' help in guiding you to abundance makes the transition from the path of lack to one of abundance a much easier journey. Your spirit team helped you create your destiny in this life. They know if you are predestined to have an abundance of money or if you've decided to experience a life of frugality. They also know if you have balanced any karma you have with money, thereby helping you to release your thoughts of lack so you can create abundance.

Your Personal Spirit Team

To learn who your guide and your teachers are, you can ask. It is that simple. Recognizing the answer is another story. For example, you can go into meditation and ask for your spirit team to show themselves to you, the area/category they will be working with you, and ask them to impress you with their names. Once they do so, write their names down and tuck them away as they rarely impress you with it twice.

Each person has the ability to draw toward them seven teachers who work with each of the psychic centers. However, we, as mortal beings, let our egos get involved. This way of working would hinder having all seven spirit teachers working with us at one time. Instead, we work on one thing to help us progress and then work on something else. We do not necessarily have all seven working with us simultaneously. Spirit teachers come in as needed or as you progress spiritually. We all have at least one. This guide is with us from birth until death. We all have a master teacher who works with our guide and teachers but not necessarily directly with us. It may not be until much later when you have progressed far enough, having worked to raise your vibration high enough to the point that your Master Teacher will come in strong enough that you will recognize him/her as being your Master Teacher.

We are each other's teachers as well. A person we run into at the mall can see truths that we may evade. The simplest phrase can clarify mounds of research. Our teachers communicate through many venues. It could be a phrase from your neighbor. It could come from a child. We learn as much from each other as we are willing to learn. To become a teacher is to share that knowledge. However, you shouldn't be casual in your sharing. To share through ego, control, or gain has karmic ramifications.

Understand that receiving guidance from our teachers is much more important than how they communicate. Be open to the messages you receive when you are working through problems. Our teachers often impress us in three different ways in an effort to get messages through to us. If your teacher cannot get the message through to you because you failed to recognize it, they can bring the message through others.

As humans, we understand so little about the conditions in which we live. With a narrow and restrictive path as our destiny, we would be helpless and vulnerable without the guidance of our teachers. We believe some of our thoughts and our wisdom are of our own creation. They are actually impressed upon us from the spirit side. Our achievements, which we think are from our own great abilities, have been aided by and promoted by spirit.

Ego can be used to our detriment. We think it is our great brain, our great wisdom, and our great abilities, when in actuality we have been guided, impressed, and led through the muck and mire by our spirit teachers. Correct use of ego is when we embrace it to set goals and rise to the challenge.

It is our love of and duty to the God-Source which brings our spirit teachers to us. There is no night or day, awake or sleeping in which your guide is not with you. Guides are the ones who create new conditions in line with the universal laws of life. Our desires may end in confusion and disaster. If we are lucky, we may see the strange forces at work saving us. We work diligently for material progress that may not be in line with our higher selves. Those situations we think will make our lives easier may in fact prove to be the worst thing that can happen to us. Having all the money you want may create a reluctance within to grow spiritually. Greed may create more negative emotions, harming your ability to view others as equals. Humankind has the tendency to interfere in others' lives because of envy, dislike, ignorance, and ego. Even what we term "positive emotions," such as admiration and love, can be harmful when we apply them to another's life.

Left to our own devices, we humans would make the wrong choices for ourselves more often than not. One of the human traits we can develop to help us navigate is accountability. Our guides and teachers help us to shoulder the responsibility of accountability. If we were, to be honest with ourselves, without our ability to be held accountable by karma, we would not be ready to progress spiritually. This would cause us to sink further into negative life experiences rather than walking the path of our destiny.

Spirit does not save us from karmically necessary shocks or disasters if those experiences will help us with our destinies. Our teachers bring strength, health, and ambition to navigate those situations our egos deem insurmountable. We are given choices or options in order to learn through experience. Spirit teachers see more clearly where opportunities for further progression lie on our paths. They work to impress us with paths that lie ahead to get us to where we need to be. What may be seen as a break in progress when we pass is not. As we go back into spirit, we can take up where we left off. There is continuity between our worlds. However, we do learn faster while on the earth plane simply because there are so many different venues from which to learn and progress.

Spirit teachers awaken within us the spiritual choices of right and wrong. Because of their willingness to serve mankind as teachers or guide, they come to it unselfishly. Our teachers see what we cannot. They know and understand the long-range ramifications where we see only the momentary highs and lows. When we make a wrong choice, they love us through it. When we overcome an impediment or learn a lesson, they celebrate.

Our first step should be to align with our teachers so our work becomes deeper and more fulfilling. When we ask for help, we call it a prayer, and they work to help us answer the prayers which are most in line with our paths. We should be aware of how we pray. As we grow spiritually, so do they. They are the messengers between us and our higher selves. Our prayers are answered in harmony with the laws and conditions of our mortal existence. Our spirit teachers open the way for us so our vision will be clear and we will come into a better, clearer communion with our higher selves, and our decisions will be more in tune with the God-Source.

The following is an outline of concepts of how your spirit team can show up. You may experience a teacher who impresses upon that you he is a Buddhist monk who would then fall into the category of "sister/nun/priest". If you are a writer, you may have a scribe show up for you. The following descriptions are guidelines to help you to understand who your spirit team is and what they will help you with.

- **The Master** - an entity or spirit who has progressed to the point of mastering life and death. Your master teacher has many students throughout the universe. They direct your guide and your teachers. They help you explicitly in your spiritual growth and development and view this development over many, many lifetimes.

- **The Chemical Doctor** - oversees the health and well-being of the physical body and assists in the development of the psychic facilities (faculties).

- **The Sister / Nun / Priest** - gives comfort and spiritual affinity in daily emotional involvement.

- **The Nurse / Doctor** - assists in emotional development and unfoldment.

- **The Native American** - gives us strength, healing, and protection. They are the masters of the natural forces who very often stand as a guide and is with us at all times. This entity also aids in the development of any healing gifts we may have predestined.

- **The Material Doctor** - gives assistance and guidance in all material and practical matters such as financial, career, and business.

- **The Doorkeeper** – entity who works with mediums and keeping them protected from any entities that are of low vibration or slows down the flow of entities who may be trying to come through so that the medium is not "overrun" with spirits.

It is important to call upon the doorkeeper for protection when doing work directly with spirit.

- **The Door Opener** - a child, usually a girl, who has passed into spirit during infancy or childhood and assists us in minor daily needs and loves to be called upon. This entity also runs messages from your spirit teacher to you and aids in psychic readings by running the messages between the reader and spirit.

Our level of progression determines how many and which teachers come through. Those who haven't predestined a psychic or heavy spiritual path will only "attract" teachers appropriate to their needs. Those not on their destiny path may only have their Native American guide working with them until such a time as they choose to go back on their path.

Prayers than can be helpful when asking for help from our guides/teachers:

"Spirit (or if you know their names address them accordingly) - if it is in my highest and best interest, I ask for your guidance and aid in _____. Thank you and so be it (or amen)."

"Spirit (or if you know their names address them accordingly) - I ask for a sign, which is so far beyond coincidence that I have absolutely no doubt the answer is from you, for help in _____. Thank you and so be it (or amen)."

INTEGRATION

Most people have been taught that Jesus is the one and only Christ. The word "Christ" is a term for the level of consciousness we strive to attain. What is meant by "Buddha will ascend the throne" is his teachings of equality will become more evident and accepted as a path to our enlightenment. In fairness, we are probably 100 years away from this starting to happen. We are still struggling with racial discrimination, as well as dogmatic and patriarchal religious teachings. The hate and division we are experiencing with each other have to be dealt with before we start to see each other as equals. Somewhere within me I am hoping it doesn't take the five generations people refer to when breaking through the family functions/dysfunctions. However, it will take something fairly cataclysmic to get all of us on the same page. There are too many people indoctrinated with fear and judgment who, in turn, are indoctrinating their children with the same. We are still torn spiritually. We worry more about how we look and being right than we worry about sharing space and giving love.

You should understand that we can choose NOT to incarnate again after this life. However, the reason we incarnate is that we can progress faster by learning lessons through an earth life than by staying in spirit and working there. You can say repeatedly you won't incarnate again. However, remember your higher self knows more clearly why you have incarnated and will make the decision to incarnate again while you are in spirit. Understand one more thing. The option to incarnate at this time offered us the ability to pay off (or bring into balance) ten times the karma than in other lives because the vibration is higher and time is moving more swiftly.

Many people will have a different take on this particular chapter. Regarding the concept of channeling angels - those who have embraced the concepts of archangels and guardian angels are still coming from the Piscean thought process and haven't let go of the concepts they were taught as children. People who are saying they are channeling these angels are reinforcing those beliefs. My thought on channeling angels is... people aren't channeling angels. The entities the channeler is bringing through are holding the energy attributed to angels and are trying to impress the channeler with the vibration but are not actual angels. However, because the person doing the channeling is still coming from the Piscean teachings, the entity is interpreted by the channeler as being an angel.

It is much more sensible for you to work with your guide and teachers who have helped you formulate your destiny plan. From the minute of conception, a vibration was sent out. You accepted the human body and created from that the circumstances of the life you now live. From the moment you accepted that human body, you put together your spirit team. You chose the family, town, and time at which you were born. How amazing is that? Your guide and spirit team have chosen to help you. They have shared mortal lives with you, and by committing to helping you, they will grow spiritually also.

As stated in the first chapters, the spirit determines the length of time it needs the human form for the incarnation they are in. The spirit has from conception up to two years to fully take on the life it has chosen. While the vibration may be perfect upon conception, situations change and the spirit may decide the physical vehicle will no longer provide a viable destiny for spiritual progression. There are many ways the spiritual being may leave the body. One is to release it to another spirit or to just leave the body. This is often the case with SIDS. The incarnating spirit may only need a few weeks/months in utero to bring about a balancing of karma for itself. A miscarriage or an abortion will satisfy this balancing of karma.

Something else you should know is that your family member who has passed is not your guide or one of your spirit teachers. You chose your team before you incarnated. Those who are on the Earth at the same time as we are cannot possibly stand as our guides. An example of this is, much as I love my son and miss him horribly, he wouldn't have incarnated to me if he was going to stand as one of my teachers. This isn't to say that he can't offer me guidance, help, or information. He can and does, especially with regard to his daughter.

CHAPTER ELEVEN

PRAYER

The God-Source does nothing but create and love. The God-Source can change the divine substance into that which we recognize as matter. From thought came the Earth. In the beginning, the God-Source, who is spirit, filled all space. When the God-Source realized who it was, it moved. God-Source withdrew within the God-Source's self until all space was empty and that which was filled was shining. This is the God-Source's light.

Think of the light as truth. Darkness is the inability to see or experience truth. Our auras reflect the truth within. Our lives are full of lessons brought through our creation to help us see the light of truth. The lessons continue and our lights will shine brighter (or dimmer) as we progress (or regress). "The truth will set us free." (John 8:32.) All of this is in line with the plan of the God-Source to experience itself. If it weren't, none of this would happen. It was a thought, an image. The thought had action by word or sound; the action was creation. "Be still and know that I am God" is well worth remembering when going into meditation. Prayer is the asking; meditation is the willingness to hear the answer.

Positivity should be maintained in everything around and through us. Our words, our thoughts, and our actions toward ourselves and others should be positive in nature. If they are not, you may be sending out negation/curses toward those you profess to love. We should always protect ourselves with the pure white light of the Christ consciousness, and then affirm that only good shall go from us and only good shall come to us. What we think (pray) should only be good. Then when it returns to us, it will be good. It is the truth of Karmic Law / the Golden Rule. We reap what we sow.

We all understand the concept of ask and ye shall receive. It is the spiritual law of supply and demand. "Ask" by use of prayer is the demand as we reach out for help. "Receive" is the reaction from the universal infinite supply. You cannot have one without the other. It is yet another expression of duality.

The supply is infinite. It does not await your worthiness; it awaits your prayer. Once you ask, you tap into a vibration that starts the flow toward you. The God-Self wants us to see the unlimited possibilities. As we unfold, the Divine unlocks the doors to the supply.

If we allow negativity or doubt to rise up within us, we create a flow of supply that is created from our negative thoughts and emotions. It effectively cuts us off of positive abundance until we realize our thoughts and emotions create our flow. If we are constantly offered help and we constantly turn it away, we are telling the universe we don't need help. If we constantly attach ourselves to dysfunctional relationships, we are telling the universe that is what we want. It is our responsibility to change the dialogue with positive thoughts, words, and actions.

It is this part of the balance humankind has struggled with. Because of the density of the earth's vibration, the flow can move slower. Our thoughts struggle with worthiness, guilt, and envy, slowing the flow to receiving the positive. While our hopes and our desires are lighting up a path to supply us with positive abundance, our negative beliefs about ourselves are like boulders or potholes in our paths. Some may think they must suffer greatly before they are deserving so they will create a venue of pain and suffering. Others may feel they are not worthy caretakers of abundance because they squandered money in the past. Others have been good stewards of the abundance but have become envious of another's life. These are all fear-based thoughts, causing us to feel negative. Fear comes before all negative emotions. Instead of feeling guilty, envious, or any other negative emotion, we should be asking ourselves, "What is it we fear?" The answer may surprise you.

If we allow the God-Self to operate within the constructs of our daily lives, meditate and follow the intuitive guidance from our spirit teachers, we will allow the divine light within to shine brighter, expressing itself more fully within our lives. It is through this we will open more fully to the divine and infinite supply.

Desire

Prayer is a sincere expression of a wish, hope, or want to bring forth or manifest that which is desired. Affirm your possession of the good that you desire and have faith that you will receive it. Once you send out the request, say "thank you" because it is already done. If the objects of our prayers are in alignment with what our higher selves have predestined to achieve, our prayers may balance any karmic debt we may have, then we will create it. Our spirit team works diligently to help us remove our blocks and balance our karma through higher awareness and spiritual progression. Their number one priority is to help us get into harmony with the God-Source so that we don't have to return to this dense plane of existence again. In that is also a warning: Be careful what you ask for because you might just get it.

True prayer is a desire that we put forth to bring about that which we feel we truly want or need. When we are not clear about our desires or when we negate our desires with fear, we lose or do not receive that which we desire. Think of desire as an experience you want to have. How it plays out depends on how you view your desires. Positivity will bring you positive experiences. Negativity will create a negative experience. The "I want" implies lack. Knowing the universe is abundant in all things allows us to remove the "I want" to "I have plenty" or I am blessed with enough. One must ask and then has to create. It is the best way for our spirit teachers and guides to answer our prayers and questions. We have to be active participants in our unfoldment.

Power

Power is the energy within that sends forth all actions from us, including our desires and fears. We grow the strength of our power within by learning truth and unfolding our spiritual gifts and knowledge. With knowledge comes a brighter light and a raising of our vibration. Power exists within all of us. This one spiritual law must, out of necessity, be combined with realization and knowledge so we don't abuse it.

Power can only manifest within ourselves through our own determination. It is not a gift that can be given by our guide or teachers. Therefore, it is a responsibility each of us must develop to its fullest. Power is invincible. We are the dynamic force in our ability to create for ourselves. When we use this power, it gives us ideas, options, and venues in order to create that which we desire and a better world for ourselves.

The God-Self is an unlimited source from which all that we desire is given. It knows in its vast array of knowledge that which we desire. It wants to give us all that we ask for, but we have to ask. Desire and power are animating, awakening principles with which we tap into the God-Self. Our ability to engage the energy of power and desire is predicated on our true desire to progress. If you place your objective within the stillness of your mind, holding that thought as perfectly clear in your mind, you have then triggered the desire. As you keep holding your thought, it will build in power. It is then you send it out as a positive life experience. Power is your spirit within the very center of your being, awaiting your desire to make it manifest through physical action.

Abuse of Power

When one person/group of people hold sway over another person/group of people and their destiny and they use that power to negatively manipulate the thoughts and actions of others, that is called abuse of power. This can be experienced to such a harmful degree it fills the hearts of those affected with fear long after the experience has ended. How, then, does the person/people who were negatively impacted recover? Meditation brings light to erase fear, but prayers to our spirit team can expedite the healing. This damage can be lessened by our willingness to take a step in the opposite direction. We cannot hide our light without it dimming. We must reach out to others, share, and grow, trusting our spirit team to guide us to truth.

In taking the words or actions of others personally, we have created an imbalance. This, too, is an abuse of power. As a victim, we can use the energy sent to us to manipulate people to our side. This is why we create our learning opportunities by drawing others forward to help us learn our lessons. When we take offense, it is showing us we have something to learn from the situation. By reacting negatively, we send out waves of anger meant to hit the other person or people. We have sent negativity out without taking responsibility for how we received their words or actions. This abuse of power is meant to bring harm to others. When we understand we are only half of the equation, then we are more likely to be accountable for our part in the interaction. You can change the direction of this imbalance by sending back love and light. This allows for the other person to either heal or move on to someone else more open to engaging negatively with them.

We cannot continually hold others accountable for our mistakes. Constantly being the victim is another abuse of power. For example, if you are asked where you would like to go to dinner and your reply is, "I don't care, wherever you want to go," then you complain you never get to eat where you want, it creates an imbalance. The person who is doing the complaining is the one who has abused the power. By handing over power, we can't complain when we don't have it.

Our egos often create abuse of power. It is never okay to step into anyone's vibration to perceive or try to intuit what they are dealing with, or feeling. Going into their energy without their permission is a violation of ethics. When we try to fix another's life or experiences, we have weakened them. We cannot presume to think we know what is best for them.

Sending people healing when they haven't asked for it or accepted it is an abuse of power. This may sound contrary to many people's beliefs as they feel it is okay to send healing. We need to understand we do not know or understand a person's destiny, nor do we know what it is he/she is working on to progress. An illness, a heartbreak, or loss of any aspect in his/her life may be predestined to help him/her learn something very important for their soul's growth. What we can do is say a prayer for their highest good. Prayer is asking, it isn't taking control. A prayer is compassionate. Leaving people to experience what they have created is also loving and compassionate.

The Master Builder Prayer

This is a prayer handed down to me as I studied at UCHS. This is an all-encompassing prayer meant to bring healing. I don't know where this prayer originated. I am introducing it as "Author Unknown," and I have made absolutely no changes, corrections, or editing to the prayer. It is as it was given to me. It also includes the five reasons to continue living.

"Thank you, Eternal Presence, for that which I am receiving now. I forgive and I am forgiven. My belief in anything other than my highest good is healed now. I accept strength and the power moving through me as perfect oneness. Echoing deep Within, I now speak with the truth I know and feel, and this truth is law and love and already has its being.

I now call upon and use this Divine Power for good and neutralize and return to the God-Source in my thoughts, speech, and actions, whatever has caused me, or appears to cause me to experience wrong or false beliefs, attitudes, expressions, experiences, opinions, thoughts, actions and illusions.

That which gives power to hurt, anger, fear, frustration, resentment, rejection, self-pity, condemnation, hate, failure, conceit, self-depreciation, comparison, arrogance, criticism, inaction, and any and all consciousness that produces confusion, lack, limitation, or, disease is now neutralized and returned to the God-Source, for I wholly accept being the God-Source's perfect expression and truth.

Whatever is necessary for me to infinitely live, love, be, and express my perfect and whole being (oneness) in the Christ consciousness is manifested in, around, through, with, and for me Now! I am guided by inner spirit to better patterns of thinking.

Here, now, the kingdom of the God-Source is revealed to me in wisdom and understanding and the divine plan for me joyfully, spontaneously, compassionately, gently, is! I accept with child-like grace. I am the living, loving, moving, acting, expressing, thinking, spirit of the God-Source, and my name in perfect harmony, peace, beauty, order, timing wisdom, understanding, youth, power, mind, soul, spirit, life, truth, love, principle, health is (insert your name).

I work perfectly with all life and things, and all life and things work perfectly with me. I accept my eternal and abundant good and blessings and impart to all living things this divine plan and awareness, this truth-law-and love. The Divine Alchemist moves and operates through and within all of me. I release and let flow to and through me this Power of Alchemy and know that forever flows this God-Substance, this something good, in, around, through, with and for me and all living things in a perfect way.

The God-Source is good - I am good. I am that I am. I accept the consciousness of the Christ and Christed Ones and speak my word that it moves and operates through all of me now! I accept what is rightfully mine and that is in my highest and best interests as a part of the whole.

Flowing abundantly in, through, around, with, and for me is the God-Source's divine radiance and love, wisdom, and understanding - that certain something I feel within and without my personal being, and I glow and am alive with this warm penetrating energy and vital life force, and impart to each living thing some part of this spirit of life - of the God-Source!

I choose to recognize and use this ability, this power of the God-Source for good within me to change negative to positive, wrong to right, illusions to truth, evil to good, disease to health, death to life, in a good God-like way. I accept my oneness with the universe. I release, relax, let go, let the God-Source, and give thanks for all good abundance, oneness, experience, and perfect balance. And So It Is. Perfect the God-Source within me, perfect life within me, which is the God-Source come forth into expression through me as that which I am; lead me ever into the paths of perfection and cause me to see only the good."

Reasons to Live and to Continue Living:
1. Clear away psychological problems
2. Abide by ethical principles
3. See to the health of the body.
4. Serve constructively in the world without ego motivation.
5. Surrender to God.

Protection Prayer

You can say this daily or when you find yourself in a conflict/combative situation

> "I am surrounded by the pure white light of the Christ consciousness. I am a Mirror of God. Only good can come to me and only good can go from me. So be it. I am a Mirror of God."

Abundance/Prosperity Prayer

> "I am surrounded by the pure white light of the Christ consciousness. I am connected to the positive flow of abundance. The universe is abundant. All that I need is available to me NOW!"

Clarity

> "I am surrounded by the pure white light of the Christ consciousness. God-Self, Creator of my life, you are my most clear advisor. Please show me a clear sign with regards to my destiny (or say the situation) and what you want me to do. I ask the sign be so far beyond doubt that I know it comes from you."

Healing

Concentrate deeply on the healing energy as it flows through you. Sometimes it will be very powerful and sometimes you will not be aware of this power, but it is always there. The more you use it, the stronger it will become. You may use the mantra at night before going to sleep to send healing out to one who needs it and asked for it or for yourself. As you give off this energy you may experience what seems like a hot flash, direct this energy into your hands.

Here are three mantras. Pick the one you feel you want to use. If none of them feel right for you, then make one up for yourself that covers what you feel is important for you.

- I Invoke the healing power of God-Source and spirit to flow through me into this vibration to heal every disease, cure every malfunction, to make this vibration healthy and strong in mind, body, and emotion. For this, I do give thanks. And So Be It.

- I Invoke the power of God-Source and spirit to flow through me into this vibration mentally, physically, and emotionally. Correcting all malfunctions, curing all sickness, illness, disease, curses, malfunctions, and dysfunctions within this vibration. I ask this request be forthcoming immediately. So Be It.

- I Invoke the Cosmic Forces of Healing and the Angelic Beings in charge of the Healing Rays to flow through this vibration mentally, physically, and emotionally, correcting all malfunctions, curing all sickness, illness, disease, curses, malfunctions, and dysfunctions within this vibration. I ask this request be forthcoming immediately, So Be It.

In the end close the healing with:

"I thank you for this perfect and instant healing. I thank you for allowing me this opportunity to serve as your conduit of this healing. Amen"

OM MANI PADME HUM

Om Mani Padme Hum
Na Ka Sa Da Na
Em Na Fa El Em Na Fa

Em He To Ba Salam
He Fa Ti Sa Ho Nunk So Nam
Bis Melima Mi Ta Heen
Om Mani Padme Hum

Om
Pronounced Aum - The practitioner's impure body, speech, and mind transform into the pureness of mind, body, and speech of a Buddha
Mani
The desire to become enlightened with truth so the mind knows no poverty
Padme
Wisdom is capable of keeping you from contradiction
Hum
Fully balanced wisdom with enlightened truth - Purity

Put together the meaning of Om Mani Padme Hum means to bring into balance all that we are dependent upon which we use to transform our mind, body, and spirit into a vehicle capable of manifesting the wisdom and truth.

Mantra
A mantra is a statement of affirmation made over and over to bring clarity and focus. It also helps us to separate our personal from the spiritual. Look at it as a repetitive prayer.

Affirmation
A statement made to confirm an ideal or intention.

INTEGRATION

Prayer is so powerful. Do you wonder why I say God-Source, True Source, or Creative Source instead of God? I shared earlier during the first chapter that we humanized the energy known as God. We gave it a personality and drew pictures of this energy as a human on a throne. Have you ever wondered why they say you cannot see God, for if you do it will kill you? It is because it is an energy that expresses as light. That doesn't mean it doesn't have consciousness. It means that we don't have the capabilities while on Earth to understand its form in its entirety. I also don't believe it has a gender, as we are the ones that split into males/females to experience life on Earth.

There are a couple of thoughts about prayer that seem conflicting. The first is "Ask and you shall receive." The second is "The most powerful prayers are those for others," Do you know why prayers aren't always answered? For the same reason prayers for others are most powerful. When we pray for ourselves, we don't always feel worthy, thereby negating our prayer with doubt.

When we pray for others, we do so out of love and desire. Love puts the power behind the prayer. When we see someone who needs help or healing, our compassion kicks in, our ego is gone, and we pray. It takes practice to do this for ourselves. It takes healing. How do we get healed? We ask for it. We pray about it, and then we meditate on it to hear the answer. The answer can guide us to someone who can help, or it can be an epiphany we need. It doesn't really matter how it comes as long as we let it come.

Sometimes what we pray for is not always in our highest interest. Understand the prayer may go out to the God-Source and that you are also praying to your higher self and your spirit team. Think about it. The God-Source gives you Free Will, has sent you out on this journey to have experiences, and loves you purely and divinely. You are it and it is you. To it, there is no bad experience, no bad lessons to be had. Everything that is experienced is an expression of the God-Source's love for us. We return so it can be made whole.

Now let's look at the "be careful what you ask for." We ask for "things" we think we need to live a full, happy, and more complete life. When we ask for those "things" such as a partner or a new job, we might just get it. However, it is not always in the way we perceive it as we create it. We consciously create everything, so if we are used to dysfunction in our home or work, instead of learning the lessons from our current situation we might get a replacement situation that may have a disastrous effect.

The moral of the story is when we pray, we will manifest a healing one way or another around that for which we pray. It isn't a bad thing. Once you understand completely how prayer works, it will work for you perfectly.

CHAPTER TWELVE

SPIRIT GIFTS

The village doctor, the midwife, the witch, the temple priest/ priestess, the mystic, the oracle, these are just some of the names that were given to people who have expressed their gifts of spirit. Over the centuries there have been many names for those who embrace their gifts of spirit. For some, those gifts come naturally from birth. Others have to work to develop their gifts. We had all those gifts and many more, then lost them when we lost our memories of our true selves and our creation. It does not matter if we call it a woman's intuition or gut feeling, those gifts, once they are developed, give us the gift of truth and a connection to our higher self, our God-Self.

Each of us has some level of ability. Each of us has come across varying opportunities to develop it further, either by sheer chance or by design. Some people who struggle with the concept of developing their spiritual gifts may not do so because they are scared or maybe they were taught by the religious doctrine of their faith that their gifts are from Satan.

Many people may not be able to develop their gifts because they abused them in a past life. To some degree, this is true only because we create our own experience of thinking negatively about our gifts of spirit. We can choose to work on developing them in this life. By choosing to do so, we should understand it is a serious undertaking, and we must take responsibility for our gifts with integrity. When doing so, you will be able to set your intentions for the correct teacher to show up to aid you in your quest.

Some people may not be able to progress as quickly as others. This is why we must choose to set in motion our desire to attract the best teachers for us. Many people take a quick weekend course for an exorbitant amount of money to develop their gifts. Unfortunately, they aren't taught that after the weekend is over the trainee needs to practice, working continuously to improve his/her skills. By training daily, the accuracy of the gift improves and the skillset keeps developing. Just taking a weekend course is not training enough for anyone to go out and start practicing for money. The people who offer these courses will still help you progress spiritually; it just may not be the way you envision. What is of major importance is the development we work toward today will help us in this life and all our lives.

For those of you who have knowledge of the Bible and are hesitant to train because of the teachings from your religious background, there are sections in the Bible that refer to these gifts. I have included an entire section called Biblical Reference at the end of this book. This reference section is meant for you to see that our gifts are positive unless we abuse our power with them.

These psychic and healing gifts are original to the spirit within all of us. This means that we had them prior to our fall. These gifts were given to us as a part of who we are, as a part of the God-Source and therefore are a part of us. They are waiting to be tapped into. Once we start bringing them forth, we open the doors to our higher selves and eventually to our subconscious and superconscious.

The correct use of the mind as an instrument of awareness makes it not only a powerful tool in our toolkit but one that increases in its ability the more it is used. By continually unfolding, we grow in potentials and opportunities. Just as we expand our education and expand our opportunities for making money, we should be expanding our gifts of spirit as far as possible, never limiting our own progression. We should never cease to reach far and wide. When we limit our perceptions, we limit our experiences.

When you decide it is an "either/or" scenario, you have placed a box around your potentialities and have accepted limitations of your possibilities. This allows for a desperate fear to take hold as your needs grow larger and your options grow smaller. Let go of your need for the safety of your box and you will see a life flowing with unlimited options from which we choose.

Healing

One of the greatest gifts to develop and master is our healing abilities. What better way to help ourselves heal and progress while helping others? Until everyone has progressed to the point of bringing self-healing, healers will be needed. There are many instruments of healing recognized today. Here is a short list:

Massage	Reiki	Polarity
Vibrational Healing	Chiropractic	Diet/Exercise
Western Medicine	Eastern Medicine	Alternative Medicine
Oriental Medicine	Herbology	Crystal Healing
Aromatherapy	Sound Therapy	Trance Healing

Jesus was recognized as the Healing Christ. He had a natural ability and understanding of how spirit could flow through him into another's vibration, curing sickness, illness, injury, malfunctions, and dysfunctions. The New Testament of the King James Bible told story after story of Jesus' miraculous healings using his gifts. What Jesus' teaching also showed us was how we can and will develop these gifts for ourselves. One of the passages is referring to what Jesus taught was "and this too you shall do"

If we fully understand the nature of the God-Source, then we unlock the key to healing. Disease is created by humans through each individual's state of mind. Only through the progress and development of our spiritual selves will disease, sickness, illness, curses, malfunctions, and dysfunctions of the body, mind, and spirit be eradicated. Our goal is to open up to unconditional love to heal ourselves. This will help us reconnect to the oneness so that nothing exists which has the power to limit or hinder us except for that which we create. Since the God-

Source is a part of us, we embody the God-Source. Combine the all-knowing intelligence with divine love and the infinity of power and you will understand the secret of healing and the secret of harmony within your life.

Intuition and Psychic Development

No one has walked the Earth without gaining something of value that will eventually carry them forward in their soul's progression. We often wonder why we have a life of strife when we work so hard to live as correctly as we think is possible. Sometimes we need our tears to fall, to bruise our knees to receive a higher truth and to light the fire which stimulates the power within to seek higher truths. It is humankind's mindset that taught us we need to create suffering to achieve. The martyr complex has been established as if it were a higher calling. We erroneously think to be worthy of our universal love we must be willing to suffer for "God." This was a carryover from the sacrificial mindset and stories of the Bible.

Intuition opens the door and lights the way for truth to come through. Our meditations give us the ability to listen to our higher selves, and our spirit guide and/or teachers. Through this guidance we learn to avoid those martyred pitfalls. While some lessons are necessary for bringing about the payment (balance) of our karmic debts, other experiences may not be in our best interest and should be avoided so as to not take us off the path of our destiny.

If we do not open to our intuition in order to better receive truth, we can be led astray by people who establish themselves in our lives as wiser and more knowledgeable than we are. Instead of us begging for guidance from someone or beating our heads against the wall worrying about what steps we should take next if we develop the skills necessary to allow the guidance to come from within, we will have much more peaceful, harmonic lives. There is no one who understands your destiny, your karmic debt, or your abilities better than the God-Source, yourself, and your spirit team.

There are many venues to open the door to your intuition. First and foremost is the development of a consistent meditation practice. Understanding and learning how to meditate will teach you to feel your own intuition, and how to work toward developing your abilities in order to help others. No one has exactly the same meditation practice. Do not worry if you do not meditate or think you should meditate like someone else. Just embrace that which helps you to learn your style and work with it.

As discussed before, there are different ways to express healing abilities. There are different approaches to developing our intuition. The ability to get into someone's vibration is the one constant truth in both healing and intuitive development. This, like meditation, takes practice. If you are looking to develop, you will be led to the right teacher.

We have different ways with which to express our intuition and to receive guidance. Here are some of the tools we have to bring forth truth through our psychic abilities:

Vibration	Psychometry	Tarot
Astrology	Numerology	Divining
Runes	Crystal Ball	Dream/Symbol Analysis

Here are the gifts of spirit that have been shown to connect to the other side:

| Evidentiary Mediumship | Physical Mediumship | Trance Mediumship |
| Direct Voice | Channel | |

Growing within your own intuition also has the effect of growing the light around you. Truth will be shown regarding situations, beliefs, patterns, people, things that are not in your highest and best interest. Hanging on to those people and situations can slow your progress, if not halt it all together. It is much wiser to remove all negation, sickness, illness, disease, curses, malfunctions, and dysfunctions, and the people/situations that manifest in your life so you can replace them with positivity, health, wealth, peace, light, love, and prosperity.

Terminology

There is a difference between psychic and mediumship gifts. The phrases used to give truth and understanding are often misused and confusing. Just what is meant when we say someone is clairvoyant?

The concept of clairvoyance has taken on the misnomer of someone seeing within their mind's eye. Then there is the misunderstanding that someone who is clairvoyant is not necessarily clairaudient, clairsentient, or a trance medium.

Clairvoyant refers to people who have their third eye open. They have the ability to actually see spirit outside of themselves and not just in the pictures within their minds. They can sometimes access the akashic records, if they have a high enough consciousness, such as the Christ Consciousness. This is not to say there aren't times in which we have flashes of clairvoyance or a clairvoyant experience. If you have seen spirits as if they are standing or sitting next to you or near you, you have the ability to open your third eye. To have the third eye opened all the time could create inconveniences in our lives as we would need assistance moving about our days without the ability to drive independently or being able to do normal tasks like cooking.

Clairaudient refers to people who have their spiritual inner ear open and can hear spirits talking outside of themselves. Most often it is just one ear that is open, not both. This is not the voice within. Sometimes you might be in the process of falling asleep and hear talking or music. I call this the "in-between world." The correct term for this is "hypnogogic state." It is the time when we don't have resistance. Some people who have been diagnosed with schizophrenia might actually be clairaudient.

Clairsentient refers to people who use their five senses psychically. The difference between a clairvoyant and a clairsentient is that a clairsentient sees pictures in their mind's eye. The sense of touch can bring the feeling of cold when spirit is near or spirit brushes against us. Clairsentients can also feel emotions. They may experience "tastes" or "smells." An example of this might be a symbol that is being given to them such as food. The clairsentient might "taste" a situation by getting a bad taste in their mouth would denote a bad situation, as well as a good taste representing a good situation. Most of us are clairsentient.

Mediums are always psychics, but psychics are not always mediums. Mediums work between this world and the spirit world (etheric). Mediums work with their spirit team to bring forth messages from their team or someone's loved one that has crossed over. There are many different categories of mediumship. It is through training that a medium finds their specialty.

Trance Medium refers to people who go into a deep, half-conscious or a self-hypnotic state where they are not affected by outside stimuli. The mediums can then open up to allow their spirit teams the use of their bodies to give messages/readings.

Physical Medium refers to people who go into a very deep trance state, they pull energy from the sitters (those in attendance), creating ectoplasm. Ectoplasm is a thick, sticky, smoky substance created from the energy of the sitters. The Physical Medium will exude the ectoplasm from his/her body and spirit will then use the ectoplasm to slow its vibration down enough to use the ectoplasm to speak to the sitters through the ectoplasm. Another example may be that spirit will step into the ectoplasm to establish a physical form. A physical medium might also use a trumpet, or have a closed box with pen and paper in it for spirit to write messages on. This is a very rare gift.

Psychic refers to people who extend their energy into the auric field of another. They will be impressed with words, symbols, concepts, and activities the other person is manifesting. They develop their understanding of the symbols and "visions" they get. This is known as their psychic vocabulary.

Channels sit with their "channel" open to receive messages from spirit. They form a direct link with a spirit to receive the messages and share them with those sitting in attendance on this side. They work with their spirit team to bring forth messages from other spirit entities. A channeler is also a type of medium. It is a very unique gift and not everyone can do it. However, in my experience, modern-day terminology has changed the concept of channeling. A channel had to practice and study for years to attain accuracy. This was accomplished by ensuring their ability to connect to a spirit entity was complete before allowing what the spirit entity was expressing was being translated accurately through the channel. Many people today are given a course in channeling and then left to work at attaining accuracy in their work, without any checks and balances. Some channels today open themselves up to whatever may be "flying by" and the messages are not always accurate.

When you train as a medium, there are always questions of accuracy, such as, how do you know with absolute certainty that what you are receiving is true or holds truth? First, it is an evidentiary gift. The entity who is coming through will impress upon the medium images of themselves or situations the sitter will remember. There are many ways the medium can show accuracy.

All gifts of spirit need training and practice. Each time you are impressed with a feeling, go with your "gut feeling," or intuition. This will deepen the relationship between you and your higher self for your intuition for yourself. By asking questions of your guide or your spirit teachers, you will be impressed with the answers. This will deepen the relationship you have with your spirit team. As you begin to trust what you are being impressed to do, say, think, and feel, you make that bond stronger. With proper understanding, use, and training you can begin to give messages for others.

The same holds true for the sitter. How, then, do you know the messages received by a psychic or a medium are accurate? While having a reading, ask yourself questions during the reading: Does this make sense to me? Does it apply to my life? Is what you're hearing reasonable? Does it sound/feel true? Is the person reading for you giving you symbols and information that resonate? This does not mean that just because they are not telling you what you want to hear that they are frauds. This means that no one can be 100 percent accurate. The symbols are for you to understand. Unless the psychic is impressed with the meaning of a particular symbol, they should leave it to you to interpret. If it is not immediately understandable to you, you can meditate upon its meaning. You also need to take responsibility for the psychic you choose to see. If you run from one to another and then yet again to another within the same day/week, you might be hearing the same information over and over again, just in a different manner. It could also be you are looking to hear what you want to hear, not what you need to hear.

Frauds are found in all fields. There is not one area in life where someone hasn't been found without the proper credentials. It is hard to ask for the credentials of a healer or psychic. There are some ways to spot frauds. Do they loop people in for more and more money? Do they set themselves up as the only way to find truth? Do they establish themselves as, "I am the only one who will or can guide/help you"? Are they operating within the parameters of the law? In other words, are they shady in their dealings?

INTEGRATION

If you are going to work on your intuitive or healing gifts, be sure to develop a regular meditation practice. Remember, not everyone meditates the same. Sometimes I engage in meditation as I walk. I am not a fan of guided meditation as a daily practice. In my opinion, listening to music all the time while meditating isn't truly getting control of your mind. It is just giving your mind something else to focus on instead of the rampaging thoughts that can run through our minds. It is far better to sit in the stillness and learn to build and hold the power within.

As I said before, I am not here to convince you. I am only sharing the training/teachings I was given. I have a friend (with whom I also work in furthering the development of my gifts) with whom I disagree in regards to the definition of clairvoyance versus clairsentient. Disagreements are created when we do not recognize each of us has our truth. Truth never changes, but our ability to comprehend it does. Do not worry if you disagree with someone over concepts or ideas in metaphysics; it is about coming to our own levels of truth.

In my training, I was taught that a clairvoyant has his/her third eye open all the time. The things the clairvoyants see through the third eye are on the outside of their bodies, not through inner visions. He/she cannot drive because a clairvoyant sees roads and people that aren't really there. This makes them quite dangerous behind the wheel. They see futuristically and into the past, never knowing if they are seeing the past, the future, or the now.

Many people presume they are clairvoyant because they get pictures in their mind's eye. I was trained that is clairsentience, which is the use of the senses to gather information. This is also the most common gift. Using our senses, much like we do every day, is the beginning of manifesting our psychic language.

Feel free to disagree with me. You have Free Will. You will believe that which holds the light of truth for you.

Ethical Use of Spirit Gifts

To fully integrate the use of our spiritual gifts, we need to hold ourselves accountable through ethical practices. Instead of making this a separate chapter, I am choosing to use it as part of the integration of our spiritual gifts.

Training

The terms "master" and "shaman" are often given as a title after a year of training. Think of the many lives you have led to getting to this moment in time. In those lives, you have spent many hours/years training in various ways. Lao Tzu once said, "The Master doesn't try to be powerful; thus, he is truly powerful. The ordinary man keeps reaching for power; thus, he never has enough." Another powerful statement that was shared with me is, "A Shaman never calls themselves a Shaman." In these two statements, we recognize the power and responsibility that goes into our training. Ethics is a very big part of that training.

Ethics in Healing Modalities

There is a reason for training. It is important that those of us who are instructors for others bring forth the highest levels of training they possibly can. We are but a stepping stone to the next level of instruction.

It is also the responsibility of trainees to choose an ethical practitioner with whom to train or apprentice themselves. If someone tells you they can train you to be a master in six months, you should question this. Our first year of training in any gift of spirit is to break down old habits, thoughts, and doubts. We should be working at shifting consciousness and reworking our vibrations by becoming healthier in mind, body, and spirit. All this is done to bring healing to ourselves.

The second year of training should be spent fine-tuning skills. For example, it is not unusual for a medium to train for three years before they begin to do readings. There is a reason for training. It is important for those who are instructors to bring forth the highest levels of training. I will repeat this over and over again. It is one of the most important lessons in becoming a teacher. People who have ill-trained another will one day have to revisit that for themselves. They will have to bring that into balance. That can sometimes be the loss of their gifts until they learn to use them correctly, or it could be that someone will not give them the truth of training.

Ethics in Aromatherapy

To be a true aromatherapist, you must study. It is important to have someone who can truly understand your medical issues before a blend can be created specifically for you. They also need the knowledge to be able to guide you in the proper use of the blend. I have been an eyewitness to people who put oils directly on the skin. Essentials should be added to a carrier oil so the oil doesn't overpower the person using the oil. If the essential oil is not added to a carrier oil, it can be very dangerous and can kick off a healing crisis.

For those who don't understand what a healing crisis is, this is when your body has such an adverse reaction that it causes the mind and spirit to crash also. Be aware that if you are getting your oils from someone who has read the pamphlet that came with the oil, the person dispensing the oil may not understand the oil they are dispensing or selling to you. This can be detrimental to other health issues you may have.

One last thing about essential oils: using too much can cause other people around you to flair up if they have a sensitivity to the oils. A drop or two through a carrier oil on the bottoms of your feet or around the prescribed area is one thing. Lathering it on can burn your skin. Having too much oil on can create issues for those people around us who don't need that particular oil. Make sure the practitioner is trained and certified in the use of oils.

Ethics in Confidentiality

Being a healer or psychic isn't about fame and fortune. However, it doesn't mean we can't earn money through the use of our gifts, as we are entitled to be paid for our time. It is important to have integrity and ethics when doing this work. This is expected of all professionals. I do take issue with people on social media talking about readings they have given. This is a breach of confidentiality. If you find someone on social media telling you about the readings he or she has done for others and you get a private reading from this person, know they will probably be talking about your reading on a public platform as well.

When someone is giving live readings, they are doing what was asked of them. We ask questions of them in public, so we need to expect to hear the answer in public. This does not cross the confidentiality integrity/ethics boundary.

Ethics in Mediumship

When someone approaches telling you that he/she has a spirit who has come in for you out of the blue and proceeds to give you the message without your approval, even without you seeking their services, this is crossing a huge boundary. No one should approach anyone giving them the information they have not agreed to get. I don't care how well-intentioned it seems. Remember, we don't always know the relationship between people. An invasive, "Hey I have your dad over here and he wants me to tell you...." may not be as well-received if that father had been abusive to them or maybe abandoned them. Worse yet is the psychic or medium that repeats your reading to others for advertising their skills. It is breaking confidentiality. I have seen this happen on social media platforms time and again. Word of mouth is your best advertising. Many readers offer live readings. Again, you lose your right to confidentiality when you ask a psychic or medium who is reading on a social media platform to read you publicly.

CHAPTER THIRTEEN

CHAKRAS

Chakras (pronounced /chaa-kruhs/) are often defined as our psychic centers of energy. In Sanskrit, chakra means wheel. They are vibratory in nature. Our chakras are linked to sound, light, colors, and vibration. They open and close with our thoughts, emotions, and experiences.

Location

There is a long-held myth that the chakras are held within our soft tissue. For example, the second chakra is often noted as being 2 inches below our belly button and 2 inches within the body. While the 2 inches below the belly button is correct, the chakra is located more inward, within the spine with the dural tube helping to feed and balance our chakra. The dural tube is filled with cerebrospinal fluid. It has its own rhythm or pulse. The main function of the cerebrospinal fluid is to provide cushioning for the brain while also acting as a shock absorber. The fluid also helps circulate nutrients and chemicals from the blood to the brain and removes the waste product from the brain.

It is this tube filled with fluid that also acts as the kundalini. The kundalini, in Yogic terms, is found at the base of the spine, or the root chakra. When activated, it is referred to as the "Fires of the Kundalini." Our chakras are opened/activated when the fires are lit. Meditation is one way to activate the Kundalini. When activated, the "serpent" uses the dural tube starting at the base of the spine. As our level of awareness rises, the chakras are activated, and our vibration rises accordingly. Spiritual awakening and unfoldment are another way to activate the Fires of the Kundalini. This rise in spiritual unfoldment can be seen as a lighting of the kundalini path through our chakras.

First/Root Chakra

The first chakra is our root chakra. When the first chakra is open, a person will feel grounded and secure. When closed, fear of being able to survive comes in. Our response of fear to a situation, be it through our mind, body, or spirit, can cause fluctuation within the chakra. The fluctuation can also be accompanied by a hormonal response. Insecurity can bring depression. If your root chakra was indeed located in the perineum, the nerve signal may or may not get to that part of the body. However, because it is located on the tip of the coccyx, the dura fluid will get the signal there quickly. Until we have reached a level of enlightenment necessary to keep them open, our chakras will open and close with the vibrational input of mind (thoughts), body, (physical), spirit (higher self).

Prana and Circadian Rhythm

As we become more enlightened, our chakras will become more stable, offering healing and stability to our earth experience. Our prana, which is defined as our lifeforce energy, is boosted and our body's circadian rhythms become stronger. Circadian rhythms influence sleep-wake cycles, hormone release, body temperature, etc. This is important to note because when they are off-kilter, the circadian rhythms have been found to be linked to diabetes, obesity, anxiety, depression, bipolar disorder, etc.

Circadian rhythms are physical, mental, and behavioral changes that roughly follow a 24-hour cycle, responding primarily to light and darkness in an organism's environment. These rhythms are found in most living things - animals, plants, and many tiny microbes. Often referred to as the "body clock," the circadian rhythm is a 24-hour cycle that tells our bodies when to sleep and regulates many other physiological processes. This internal body clock is affected by environmental cues, like sunlight and temperature. If we are out of sync with our circadian rhythms then our chakras may be affected.

Nadis and Prana

All nadis are said to originate from two areas within the body: the heart and an egg-shaped bulb in the pelvic area. Nadis are energy channels that carry the prana, (chi, Japanese, or qi, Chinese), that connect the chakras and run throughout the body. The main nadis are Pingala, Sushumna, and Ida. They run from the base of the spine to the top of the head. They are sometimes viewed as not only running through the skin but also thought to extend out to the borders of the aura.

Emotions or Behaviors and Chakras

Pride, envy, wrath, gluttony, lust, sloth, and greed are the seven deadly sins spoken of in Judeo-Christian teachings. These "sins" are generally in evidence when the chakras are closed. Removing these actions will help to keep our chakras clear and our spiritual progression flowing upward.

Chakras and DNA

Some miscellaneous information that may be useful is to note is that the symbol for DNA, the double helix, is very similar to the symbol of the fires of the kundalini. It is the flowing in and around that brings the similarity to mind.

I offer here basic information on the chakras. It is important to understand the personality traits associated with the open and closed states of chakras. Please note in this section I have changed the wording from "open" and "closed" to "positive" and "negative." I did this because closed denotes the concept there is no movement. This isn't true. Whether our chakras are in the open/positive flow or the closed/ negative flow, there is still movement, an ebb and flow, if you will. Our thoughts govern the movement.

1ST CHAKRA –

Prostate Plexus – Hindu Name – Muldahara – Root Chakra – Located at the point of the coccyx, just above the anus and genitalia.

Mantra: In conscious union with the Divine Life Force, I express the radiant light of love and divine life.

Color - Red

Element - Earth

Number of Lotus Petals - 4

Musical Note - C

Sound - La

Gland: Male testes; female ovaries

Turns - Clockwise when flowing in the positive

Positive - A person will feel life is supported and grounded; the world is a great place to be; life is complete; feel connected to Earth and nature.

Negative - A person will feel a chronic sense of fear and lack of security; feel threatened; the world is against them.

Purpose: Corresponds to basic life force. Gives us our connection to the Earth; survival.

Security, and basic human potentiality. The kundalini lies coiled at the point of the coccyx, waiting to uncoil and bring humans to their highest potential. No gland is placed here but it is said it relates to inner adrenals and adrenal medulla. Muscles in this area bring ejaculation. It also relates to sperm and ovum, which also lie coiled, waiting to spring forward and bring forth fully developed humans.

2ND CHAKRA –

Epigastric Plexus - Hindu Name - Svadisthana - Sacral/Pancreas - Located two inches below belly button directly back.

Mantra: In conscious union with the Supreme Power, I manifest spiritual strength.

Color - Orange

Element - Water

Number of Lotus Petals - 6

Musical Note - D

Sound - Va

Gland - Pancreas

Turns - Counter-clockwise when flowing in the positive

Positive - A person shows strength and vitality. There is a sense of aliveness that comes from a healthy relaxed body. Gut instincts (intuition) will be more accurate. More in touch with the feeling of creativity.

Negative - A person is uneasy, tense, and critical. Sexual energy is reduced. Life feels stiff and uncompromising. Reluctance to have sex or it may not be fully integrated with the rest of the body; sex will feel more like a purely physical function.

Purpose: - *Creative & sexual center; basic life force changed into humanity; clairsentient.*

Relates to intuition, emotion, sexuality, and creativity. Corresponds to testes or ovaries which produce various sex hormones in the reproductive system and can cause dramatic mood swings.

3rd CHAKRA –

Solar Plexus - Hindu Name - Manipura - Solar Plexus - Located on the spine behind the "dip" or hollow of the abdomen on the diaphragm also referred to as the Solar Plexus.

Mantra: In conscious union with the Divine Mind, I manifest the light of spiritual substance.

Color - Yellow

Element - Fire

Number of Lotus Petals - 10

Musical Note - E

Sound - Ra

Gland - Adrenals

Turns - Clockwise when flowing in the positive

Positive - A person is the master of their emotion, calm, brave. In relationships, it is important the third chakra remain open so both partners will feel they are masters of their emotions and capable of being equal partners.

Negative – Can't share; creativity is stifled; emotions are shut down; coward (as in yellow belly); fear governs actions; sex feels threatening; difficulty letting go and receiving; difficulty digesting food and possible weight problems.

Purpose: Energy distribution; personal power; identity/tribe; the point where creativity is manifested; our power in regards to who we are and what we express.

Relates to energy, assimilation, and digestion. Corresponds to the pancreas, outer adrenals, and adrenal cortex. These glands play a valuable role in the digestion and conversion of food into energy.

4TH CHAKRA –

Cardiac Plexus - Hindu Name - Anahata - Heart - Located at the nipple line on the sternum.

Mantra: I am one with the radiant light of Divine Love, joy, and bliss within me.

Color - Green

Element - Air

Number of Lotus Petals - 12

Musical Note - F

Sound - Ya

Gland - Thymus

Turns – Counter-clockwise when flowing in the positive

Positive - Sense of being in love; universal love; peace and well-being; finding a way to feel the feelings of "being in love" without having to have someone else trigger this joy.

Negative - Can't feel love; angry; feelings of being cut off and closed off; want to protect self from pain; the sense of not wanting to be vulnerable or to commit; a very lonely place.

Purpose: Connection between lower & higher self; connects the lower and higher related chakras; is the meeting point between mortal and spirit self.

Relates to love, equilibrium, and well-being. Related to the thymus gland. The organ is part of the immune system and endocrine. Produces T-cells for fighting off disease and is adversely affected by stress.

5ᵗʰ CHAKRA –

Pharyngeal Plexus- Hindu Name - Vishuddha - Throat - Located right below the Adams apple. Relates to communication and growth. Connected to the thyroid gland, which is responsible for growth and maturation.

Mantra: I am one with the Supreme Shakti, the power within me

Color - Blue

Element - Ether

Number of Lotus Petals - 16

Musical Note - G

Sound - Ha

Gland - Thyroid

Turns - Clockwise when flowing in the positive

Positive - Articulate; allows you to express freely; being heard; words flow in unison with the mind and spirit.

Negative - Stops your voice/can't get your point across; stutter; inarticulate; resentment. If you stop your voice, you will negate this chakra.

Purpose: Communication; finding your intellectual/philosophical voice and singing it out loud.

Relates to how we communicate with one another. Gives voice (power) to positive or negative thoughts, feelings, and actions.

6ᵀᴴ CHAKRA –

Mid-Cerebrum - Hindu Name – Ajna –Third Eye – Located in the Pineal Gland, Center of Forehead

Mantra: I am Spirit Divine, I connect with the radiant light of divine truth, wisdom, bliss, and perfection within me

Color - Indigo/Purple

Element - Thought

Number of Lotus Petals - 2

Musical Note - A

Sound - Ohm

Gland – Pineal

Turns –Counter-clockwise when flowing in the positive

Positive - Peace; intuitive sight/clairvoyant; if the third eye is open, a person can see spirit. They can see as if the past or future is happening now; (however, having the chakra open doesn't necessarily mean the third eye is); trust instincts; intuition.

Negative - People will rely too much on logic; always in their head; hard to see the MAGIC in life; difficulty making decisions; over-dependence on other people as we don't have an inner sense.

Purpose: Inspiration, insight, intuition, clarity, vision. The third eye is able to see into Akasha records; clairvoyant.

Relates to time and awareness of light. The pineal gland is light sensitive, produces the hormone melatonin, regulates going to sleep and awakening also produces trace amounts of the psychedelic chemical dimethyltryptamine.

7TH CHAKRA –

Crown aka Master Chakra - Hindu Name - Sahasrara – Location, top of head and around the sides.

NOTE: The Crown of Thorns was placed on Jesus' head to affect his connection in a negative way to his higher self and the universal mind.

Mantra: I am Spirit Divine, I am one with the radiant light of divine truth, wisdom, bliss and perfection within me.

Color: Violet/White – The light is often seen as a halo. People with their head chakra open have a direct connection to the universal mind, they are thought to be "angels of God"

Element - Enlightenment

Number of Lotus Petals – 1,000

Musical Note - B

Sound - MM.

Gland - Pituitary

Turns - Clockwise when flowing in the positive

Positive - A person will walk in the light; brings light. A person who has their crown chakras open, their words seem to spark truths within you. Naturally magnetic personality. Draws you closer to hear them, be near to them. The person will be concerned with global spiritual growth, not just personal needs; will not try to control another's beliefs.

Negative - May have had negative experiences with religion that they will equate with spirituality. The spirituality within the child may have been silenced as a child. If closed the person will have an "it's all about me, now" persona. May have had a serious injury to the head as well (this will affect the crown chakras). The energy of the crown chakra may either flow in the positive within or flow negative direction continuously). Will try to control everyone, everything, every situation around them.

Purpose: God consciousness; connection w / the bigger picture; connection to the divine oneness; link to the universe.

Connected to the pituitary gland that controls most other endocrine glands. Often called the Master Gland. It connects to the rest of the system through the hypothalamus which controls it.

INTEGRATION

It is important we have an understanding of the chakras if we are to understand when we are in or out of balance. Again, instead of saying open or closed, I referred to them as in the positive or negative flow. I don't believe they are ever closed. They are just flowing in reverse. Understanding the personality traits that go with the positive/negative flow allows us to understand where we are or where someone else is coming from regarding behaviors and emotions.

It also is great insight when we notice the shifts from positive to negative flow. We begin to understand what triggers us. Please refer to Chapter 4 — Johari's Window - for understanding how we can find our behaviors with the help of others.

When you go to have your "chakras balanced" or "aligned," think twice before doing so. As you read in the information offered above on the chakras, our chakras flow positively and negatively in accordance with our thoughts and emotions. When we have no fear or negative emotions within us, our chakras will be flowing in the positive flow, or what people like to think of as open. Life happens quickly and suddenly. Our thoughts switch from positive to negative frequently throughout our day. Let's say you just had your chakras balanced. You walk out to your car (or into the kitchen) and almost fall. Your heart flutters and you think of what might have happened had you fallen. Fear sets in. Your chakras become out of balance.

It takes a lot of work, healing, and meditation to stay in the positive flow. This is why a strong meditation practice is imperative for balanced chakras. Any life experience can affect them until we attain higher levels of awareness and we unfold in the ways of spirit. When our chakras are strong and flowing and our kundalini is activated, we are emitting the very bright light of our spiritual beingness, the metaphysical body of light and love.

BIBLICAL REFERENCES OF SPIRIT GIFTS

ASTRAL PROJECTION – *II Corinthians 12:2-3*

CLAIRVOYANCE – *John 4:17-18; Mathew 6:22; Luke 11:34*

COMMUNICATIONS IN DREAMS BY SPIRIT – *Genesis 28:12; Genesis 37:5-9; Genesis 41:1-8; Job 33:14-17*

GIFTS OF HEALING – *Numbers 28: 8-9; I Kings 17:17-24; II Kings 5:1-14; Mathew 10:1-8; Luke 14:2-4; Mark 3:2-3; John 4:47-54; John 9:1-7; Acts 9:1-7; I Corinthians 12:9; I Corinthians 12:28*

GIFTS OF SPIRIT – *I Corinthians 12:8-31*

GOLDEN RULE / KARMA – *Matthew 7:12*

INDEPENDENT WRITING / SPIRIT WRITING – *Exodus 24:12; Exodus 31:18; Deuteronomy 5:22; Deuteronomy 9:10*

INDEPENDENT VOICES – *Genesis 3:8; Genesis 15:12; Deuteronomy 9:12-13; I Samuel 3:4; I Samuel 3:10; Ezekiel 1:28; Job 33:14; Matthew 17:5; John 12:28-30; Acts 9:3-7; Acts 11:7-9*

SPIRIT WRITING – *Daniel 5:5*

LEVITATION BY SPIRIT – *I Kings 18:12; Ezekiel 3:12-14; Ezekiel 8:3; Acts 8:39*

MATERIALIZATION (seeing of spirit on the earth plane) – *Genesis 18:1; Genesis 32:24; Exodus 24: 10-11; Ezekiel 8:3; Ezekiel 11:1; Mark 16:9-12; Luke 24:15; Luke 24:30-31; John 20:12; John 20:19; John 21:1; Matthew 17:3*

MEDITATION (THE GOD WITHIN) – *Matthew 6:1-6*

ORIGIN OF MAN / DESTINATION OF MAN – *John 3:13*

PROPHECY – *Joel 2:28; I Corinthians 12:10; I Corinthians 12:28; I Corinthians 14:1-5; I Corinthians 14:24; I Corinthians 14:29-33;*

REINCARNATION – *John 3:3-14; John 9:1-3; Matthew 11:13-14; Matthew 16:13-16; Matthew 17:9-13; Revelation 3:12;*

TRANCE – *Genesis 15:2; Daniel 8:18; Daniel 10:9; Acts 9:3-9; Acts 22:17; Revelation 1:10*

TRUMPET SPEAKING – *Exodus 19:13; Exodus 19:16; Exodus 19:19; Exodus 20:18; Revelation 1:10*

Made in United States
Orlando, FL
14 November 2022

24532683R00085